SING
AND SHINE ON!

An Innovative Guide to Leading Multicultural Song

SING
AND SHINE ON!

An Innovative Guide to Leading Multicultural Song

Nick Page

Illustrations by Kathleen Tighe Clark

World Music Press

World Music Press
Intercultural Understanding through Music
PO Box 2565
Danbury CT 06813-2565 USA
Printed in the USA in accordance with all NAFTA regulations.

Cover and chapter openers designed by: Claudia Chapman.
Edited by: Lisa A. Barnett
Text designed by: Jenny Jensen Greenleaf

Every effort has been made to contact the copyright holders for permission to reprint borrowed material where necessary. We regret any oversights that may have occurred and would be happy to rectify them in future printings of this work.

The author and publisher wish to thank those who have generously given permission to reprint borrowed material:

"Thula Klizeo" by Joseph Shabalala. Reprinted by permission of Right Side Management and Joseph Shabalala.
"Cadima" (adaptation of "Kadima") used by permission of Ella Jenkins, Ell-Bern Publishing Company, Chicago IL 60614.
"Building Bridges" composed by the women of Greenham Common peace encampment in England in 1983. Melody transcription by Elizabeth Cave. Reprinted from *Rise Up Singing: The Group Singing Songbook* by Peter Blood and Annie Patterson. Used by permission of the publisher, Sing Out Publications.
"There's a River Flowin' in my Soul" by Rose Sanders, as sung by Jane Sapp. Used courtesy of Rose Sanders and Jane Sapp.
"The Duchess at Tea" by Pat Shaw. Used by permission of Chris Shuldham-Shaw.
"Dowidzenia" by Andrea Schafer © 1996 Andrea Schafer/World Music Press. Used by permission.
"La Macchina del Capo" from Welcome to Mussomeli: Children's Songs from an Italian Country Town by Rosella Diiliberto, published by World Music Press, used by permission.
"Amigos" a song of friendship by Judith Cook Tucker © 1983, 2001.

Library of Congress Cataloging-in-Publiation Data
Page, Nick.
     Sing and shine on! : an innovative guide to leading multicultural song / by Nick Page ;   illustrations by Kathleen Tighe Clark.
       p. cm.
       Includes bibliographical references.
       ISBN 0-937203-95-5
       1. Singing—Instruction and study—Juvenile. 2. School music—
  Instruction and study. 3. Multicultural education. 4. Cross-cultural orientation. I. Clark,   Kathleen
Tighe. II. Title.

Contents

Preface

· THIS BOOK is for teachers: classroom teachers, math teachers, summer camp teachers, religious school teachers, and yes, music teachers. It has been written because I feel that, more than ever before, there is a need for more singing in our schools and cultural institutions. It is extremely important that we sing. New research in a variety of fields shows exciting and important proof of music's many powers to shape and charge our minds, bodies, and spirits (Gilmore, Madaule, and Thompson 1989, 17–23, 33–37).

There is a popular saying from the African nation of Zimbabwe, "If you can talk, you can sing. If you can walk, you can dance." To this, I would add, "If you can sing, you can lead a song. If you can dance, you can lead a dance."

I am fortunate in that I work with both children and their teachers. I teach teachers to teach songs. Most of the teachers I work with believe that their students are amazing and wonderful. These teachers dedicate their lives to inspiring children to learn, to grow, and to be amazing. And yet the most common reaction I hear from teachers is, "I'm not a good singer. I can't lead songs." In this I hear, "The children are amazing, but I'm not."

There is usually a reason for this reaction. If I probe politely enough, I usually find that at some time in their youth, these teachers were told that they had no talent. It could have been a fellow student laughing at a crack in the voice. It could have been a well-meaning adult, under pressure to put on a good show, who told the young would-be teacher to "mouth the words."

We are all far more amazing than we realize. This book should be sub-titled, ''It's Okay To Be Amazing!'' because it is a theme that runs through-out. Being amazing entails feeling confident. When I lead sing-alongs, I begin with a song that I know everyone can sing well. By singing the song well, everyone gains a sense of confidence that they might not have had before. I then build on this confidence by doing what everyone might have thought impossible moments before, like singing in harmony, adding different rhythms, or dancing. I make sure that everyone feels total confidence with each of these additions. Faces begin to brighten and eyes begin to shine with a new sense of wonder—everyone is literally in awe of the amazing sound that they are making and the power they are creating. This power is the power that every community makes when voices are united in song. It is not a hierarchical power where one singer is superior to another, but rather a communal power—different voices coming together to create a harmony. People leave the sing-along with the realization that we are far more amazing than we realize.

The book is divided into three parts, *what*, *how*, and *why*. Part 1 examines the power of singing from both the cultural and physical perspectives. Part 2 is an in-depth explanation on how to teach songs and how to make the songs as powerful as possible. Part 3 is a summary explaining why singing and music are so important to both education and life itself.

Our culture makes a huge division between the talented and the untal-ented. It is assumed that if you are untalented, you should keep your mouth shut and sit still. Like a gospel preacher I shout out, ''There are no untalented people! Miracles abound in every breath: Hallelujah! Be amazing! Sing!''

I believe that singing makes us amazing. Every culture on the planet sings as a means of celebration—in every phrase saying, ''This is who I am!'' This song creates a sense of identity; it brings us together. We are all different, but by singing this song we create a harmony from our differences. Singing this song makes us powerful!

You will learn where to find powerful songs. Cultural traditions *charge* songs with amazing energy. The charge comes from the sense of identity the song creates. When a song connects us emotionally with a culture, the deep-rooted traditions of that culture add meaning to the singing. This under-standing can be like a lightning bolt, energizing the emotions—like a battery charging the soul. Children need not sing generic songs. They can sing songs steeped in tradition, steeped in power. In the folk music process, you, the song leader, will learn to own the song and make simple changes to give a folk song more power.

There are simple procedures to follow to insure great singing from all. Children can sound wonderful. All hearing children can sing in tune. All children can sing with fire. It is essential for children to sound fantastic. No one, no matter what age, enjoys doing things in a lackluster way. It really doesn't take that much effort to create excellence in singing. You get what you ask for. It's that simple. Knowing what to ask for is part of what this book is all about.

I propose that all students and teachers at every school gather once a week in a joyous all-school singing celebration. Celebrations bring students and teachers together in a disciplined and fun way, creating a positive bond between the students and their learning environment.

Every teacher can enhance her or his curricula by teaching songs. Singing can enhance the studies of other cultures. Singing strengthens listening, which then strengthens every activity from silent reading to group discussions. Singing charges the brain, increasing children's learning potential. Singing helps stimulate the desire to learn, and singing helps to form strong communities.

Let go of any fear you might have about singing. We can shine with an amazing light that is at its brightest when we join voices in harmony. I have seen thousands of people of all ages transformed by music's powers, powers they did not know were inside them.

It's okay to be amazing!

I want to thank my parents, Janet and Bill Page, as well as Dale Lyle, Kathy Clark, Harriet Hart, Lisa A. Barnett, Michael Ginsberg, Lorraine Page, Nancy Langstaff, and the many musicians, friends, and family members who helped to shape this book.

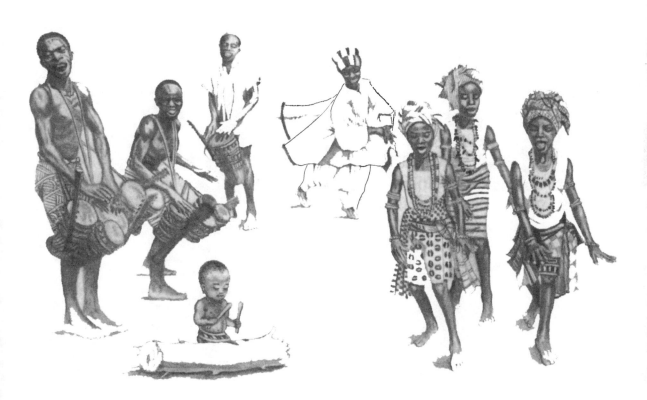

What Is
The Power
Of Singing?

We All Can Sing with Power

· I SPENT four years teaching music at a K-8 elementary school in Cambridge, Massachusetts. Preparing for my first meetings with students was exciting because it gave me the chance to set my personal goals for the children. I had previously spent three years working with a professional children's chorus in Illinois, the Chicago Children's Choir. I had learned from the Chicago experience that children, when they sing in tune, with energy and confidence, can be spellbinding. I had learned that one of the ways of making them sound good was to make them feel good about themselves. The irony was that in order for them to feel good about themselves, they had to sound good. Like the hesitant teachers I mentioned in the preface, the children needed occasional reminders about their amazing abilities.

My experience in Chicago was excellent training for teaching at the elementary school in Cambridge. On my first day, the fifth and sixth graders reluctantly came to the music room to meet the new teacher. I had set certain goals for the students. As the students entered the room, I reviewed the goals in my mind. I wanted these students to have a strong respect and appreciation for all music from all cultures, and I wanted them to appreciate their own creative powers as human beings. I knew that in order to accomplish these tasks, they had to fully participate in music making through singing—singing that would set their minds and bodies on fire, that would make them shine with energy.

I began by teaching a simple yet exciting song called "Thula Klizeo" (see chapters 6 and 11 for a transcription of the song). I explained that the song was from South Africa and that it meant "Be still my heart, even here I am at home." I talked about its composer, Joseph Shabalala, who led the group Ladysmith Black Mambazo that had toured and recorded with the pop singer Paul Simon. I explained all this with great energy, hoping that some of the energy would then be reflected in their singing. It was not. The girls, and most of the boys, sang with embarrassed, breathy tones. Four or five boys sat with clenched jaws.

I stopped the singing, which pleased the students greatly. I said nothing for a moment. Then, with a big smile, I surprised them all by saying that in thirty minutes they were going to sound great and that in two months they were going to sing in front of the entire school; they were going to sound amazing, they were going to be singing in tune with harmony, and everyone in the school was going to be amazed by their energy. Furthermore, I told them I expected a standing ovation from the rest of the school.

Experience had taught me that these statements would come true if I made them come true. All people of all ages are born with the amazing ability to do amazing things, and one of these amazing things is the ability to sing in tune, with harmony, and with energy and confidence. Good singing makes us powerful. Poor singing drains us of power. We must insist on good singing at all times. When done with energy and confidence, singing becomes an exciting activity—one that all students can look forward to doing.

Thirty minutes into the class, the students felt a new power they hadn't known before; two months later they were standing up at the Thanksgiving assembly singing "Hava Nashira," a Hebrew round, in three parts. They sang in tune, with energy. And, yes, people were amazed, none more so than the students themselves. The ovation was tremendous. I could see the students' postures straighten as they fed on this admiration, letting it fill them with confidence.

They walked off that stage with a new kind of power. They did not receive the standing ovation I had asked for, so I let them know afterward that it was still expected of them. They were in the seventh and eighth grades when it finally happened. They performed songs from many cultures ranging from antiapartheid chants to English madrigals. A goal had been met. It was one of the most satisfying moments I have ever experienced.

In Part 2 of this book, I will tell the story of how these students attained the goal of being great singers. I will explain how any teacher can lead songs successfully, provided he or she has the confidence to expect miracles.

Part 1 of this book is a song in praise of miracles—in particular, the miracle of singing. I have gained a powerful philosophy regarding music making. The story of how this philosophy evolved is important in understanding the nuts and bolts as well as the spirit of song leading. Having a goal in mind gives purpose to the mechanics.

It is sad to think of the number of emotionally wounded adults in North America who were denied the power of singing as children. They were told or somehow became convinced that they were bad singers and could not sing in tune. As adults, they still carry this scar. Most elementary school choral directors have stopped screening "bad singers" from their choral groups. In my three years with the Chicago Children's Choir, I was guilty of the crime of screening "bad singers." I can still see the hurt faces of the children who were not chosen for the school chorus. I now insist that every child can sing wonderfully, that every classroom can become a fantastic singing group, and that every teacher can become a great song leader.

What caused my change of heart? I attended a workshop with an amazing song leader named Ysaye Maria Barnwell of the group Sweet Honey In The Rock. Most of my fellow participants had never sung before or had been told as children not to sing because their voices were inferior. Ysaye taught us Zulu chants, spirituals, gospel songs, and civil rights chants—all compassionate music from the African and African American traditions. We sounded amazing singing four-part harmony, our voices ringing with resonant energy. I saw and felt the reactions of people who had, for the first time in their lives, discovered magnificence within themselves. There were tears of sadness from people who seemed to mourn the many years they had lived without sensing this power, and there were tears of joy from people reveling in their newfound magnificence. I left the workshop with a firm determination that we all had the right to live up to our full potential as humans.

I now travel throughout North America leading workshops and sing-alongs. I constantly hear of school boards eliminating much-needed music and art programs in an effort to cut costs. A frequent excuse for this is that students need to spend more time studying academic subjects and, therefore, less time on "luxuries" such as the arts. How sad. By cutting music and the arts they inadvertently undermine the academic studies they wish to support.

I have visited schools that have had no arts programs. These schools seemed lifeless, totally devoid of energy. When I asked the students if they liked the school, they usually said they didn't. There was nothing to identify with, nothing to create a sense of community or of *school spirit*. Discipline was a major problem at these schools. Children had no positive vent for their boundless emotional energy. Their emotions came out in negative ways.

Teachers labeled many of the students as *slow* learners. The word slow is important here. It refers to speed. Speed refers to how fast or slow a rhythm or pulse is moving. We are surrounded by rhythms all the time. A student's day is full of repetitions that ultimately form a rhythm. The so-called slow learners were actually students who were out of sync or out of rhythm. There was no rhythm to their learning patterns.

I consulted some teachers at a Watertown, Massachusetts, school to help them make music a daily part of each child's life. One teacher went so far as to have her students make percussion instruments. For ten minutes every day, the students would simply drum. The results were amazing. The students became more attentive. They finished their tasks with greater speed and efficiency, and they had a renewed confidence in both their play and their work. Their rhythm of learning had been enhanced by the rhythm of the drums. If this sounds far-fetched, I invite you to read on.

I began this chapter by speaking of the fifth and sixth graders who resisted singing. Two years later, they were each far more powerful human beings, confident in their creativity and proud of their abilities. By singing, we make the world a more beautiful place. By singing, we make ourselves stronger both as individuals and as members of communities. We all know the words to the African American spiritual: "This little light of mine, I'm gonna' let it shine." This light is far brighter than we have ever imagined. Through singing, people can shine with a power equaled only by supernovas. As educators, we have a responsibility to enable all students to shine with the pure radiance of creation. Hallelujah! I'm gonna let it shine!

Sing and shine on!

The Powers
of Music

···················· WE HAVE all seen children exhilarated by music—entranced by music's magnificent powers. Why are we affected like this? What are the powers of music? This question needs to be answered in order to understand why music is essential for education. To find part of the answer, I have researched two current perspectives in education, the multicultural and the multiple intelligences movements. Both are old movements that continue to evolve, and both are part of the broader perspective of holistic thinking—looking at the whole picture rather than its separate parts. Many people think of the word holistic in reference to holistic medicine, but the word applies to any perspective that values the whole picture as opposed to its pieces. When we use the holistic approach in examining the powers of music, it simply means that we wish to view music from many perspectives.

Making sense of these many perspectives is what this chapter is all about. But all the written material in the world will not convince you of music's power. *You have to experience it*. You have to feel it. You may find it necessary to go ahead to the second part of this book so you can learn how to lead songs and how to make music powerful. If you return to this chapter, keep in mind that the powers of music must be felt to be understood—felt in all dimensions: emotional, physical, and if I dare say so, the spiritual— the dimension that connects us with all things. I wrote this chapter out of a tremendous need to understand in my mind what my heart already knew.

Researchers are learning about fascinating new powers attributed to singing and music; powers that can enhance education dramatically. The wonderful irony is that these new powers aren't really new at all. Cultures around the world have been aware of music's many powers for thousands of years (Dissanayake 1988, 62–63, 158). Scientific research is now uncovering information that these cultures, not steeped in the scientific process of Western culture, already knew.

A Simple Definition of Multicultural Education

The multicultural movement evolved from the civil rights movement as a way to include diverse cultural perspectives into what was previously a single-cultural approach to education. At first, this meant integrating the African American perspective into mainstream education. Eventually, women's groups, disabled rights groups, gay and lesbian groups, and ethnic groups from the Hispanic, Asian, Native American, and many other communities added their voices to the multicultural movement.

There were two goals of this movement. The first was to teach students and faculties to honor diverse ways of cultural thinking. This evolved from a nonracist approach to a more activist, antiracist approach. The second goal was to provide, for the first time, learning environments in which diverse cultures could find their own identities at all levels of education. It was important that students be proud of their heritage and feel comfortable sharing it with others.

The acceptance of diversity does not always come easy. It is very easy to assume that our worlds or our cultures are like everyone else's world and culture, but this is not always so. Christmas, for example, is not everyone's holiday. As a religious holiday, Christmas has no place being the centerpiece of winter assemblies in the public schools. As someone who celebrates Christmas, I understand why many teachers and parents feel uncomfortable when they are asked to remove all Christian content. It is difficult to let go of the assumption that Christmas is not a holiday for everyone. When we embrace cultural diversity, on the other hand, we see a world of many celebrations, each honoring its own traditions in its own ways, whether the celebrations are religious holidays like Hanukkah, Midwinter, and Christmas, or cultural holidays like Kwanza or New Year's Day. Honoring diversity means accepting the fact that we are all different and that that is good. Human differences should no longer be seen as threatening. Human diversity does not make us weaker—it makes us stronger.

Current thinking in multicultural education has become multifaceted—looking at the whole picture of education and giving an equal and fair education to all concerned. This has meant the inclusion of special needs students in the mainstream classroom. And it has meant a rethinking of the entire educational system, ranging from curriculum and grades to discipline and learning styles.

We are still in the beginning stages of making education multicultural. Many teachers, parents, and administrators, not to mention students, are having difficulty dealing with reformists they consider to be on the radical fringe. The term *political correctness* is sometimes used to describe the thinking processes of these so-called radicals. Others are frustrated by an educational system that they consider deadlocked in ancient practices that do nothing to fight racism nor honor diversity.

From my perspective, we still haven't answered some core questions pertaining to multiculturalism. The main question I ask concerns an apparent disparity. If we are to become truly inclusionary and allow children to shine in their own way, then why do we still perceive such huge divisions between those with talent and those without? Why is the child who flunks math still considered a failure when she paints portraits like a wiz? Why is the emotionally charged child labeled a "problem child" when he is the star performer in the school's annual musical production? Why do we still accept the concept of tone deafness, when most trained teachers can teach a hearing child to sing in tune?

One might argue that these issues pertain more to the area of multiple intelligences and not to multiculturalism. I would argue that they pertain to both. Furthermore, they are issues that relate to a deeper problem—our world paradigm, our way of thinking about the world. We incorrectly believe that there is a huge gap between the talented and the untalented because we also believe in a world that is hierarchical with the strong on top and the weak on the bottom. Our model of the world is based on outdated concepts and beliefs. For example, Darwin's theory of evolution still stands, but his concept of the survival of the fittest, which has provided the basis for our modern industrial and educational systems, is being challenged by current research. A new model is emerging wherein cooperation plays an equal role with competition, where there is an interdependence of living systems, and where there is an inherent creativity (Swimme 1984, 111–39) and altruism (Wilson 1978, 149–67) in nature (Sahtouris 1989, 25).

The old paradigm embraces hierarchical thinking, which is at the heart of racism, sexism, and all the other classifications that place one group above another (Capra 1982, 21–49). The new paradigm embraces interdependence and diversity. There is no place for racism nor sexism within such a perspective.

I wish to propose a new model for multicultural education. It is a model that applies to the multiple intelligence model as well. The new model is based on our new view of nature and the world. Some call it the "New Story"; and in this story, music is of central importance—important for the body, mind, and soul—for education, and for our continuing cultural renewal.

A Simple Definition of
the Multiple Intelligence Perspective

Researchers are showing what many intuitive teachers have known all along—that traditional education works for some, but not for all. As in the multicultural movement, there is a new emphasis on reaching every child. And with this has come the realization that every child learns differently. This means that different ways of learning need to be used in the classroom—learning through movement, through singing, through touching, and through all forms of play. Terms such as *musical intelligence, emotional IQ*, and *whole language learning* have now become common.

The more ways of learning are used in education, the more effective that education becomes (Gardner 1993, 5–37). This includes the intelligence of the body—the memory of movement. It includes spatial intelligence—the ability to perceive and draw objects. The ability to work with others is now seen as essential along with the old way of learning by oneself. Reading, writing, and math skills are still vitally important, but now they are supported by the other ways of learning.

As a music teacher, I feel I have been successful in using both multicultural approaches and multiple intelligence. I have taught songs from many cultures in many languages. I have taught music using dance, hand signs, play, and improvisation. I strongly believe that as a result of this kind of singing, my students have done better in math, reading, and their other academic studies. Researchers at the University of California at Irvine have documented a powerful link between music and math studies. The ability to solve math problems is enhanced by the ability to organize sounds in the brain (Rauscher et al. 1994).

Whenever I teach a song, I give as much of a background to the song as I can. Who wrote it? When? Why? From what culture does the song come? What are the musical traditions in that culture? By giving students a deep awareness of these traditions, I have given them the chance to form emotional attachments to the music. This bonding with the music and the cultural traditions behind the music has helped to redefine who the students are as individuals and as members of broader communities. Thus, the identities of these students have been strengthened and broadened by their embracing of many powerful musical traditions. Their sense of community has been strengthened, and they have learned that their voices will always be heard within whatever community they find themselves.

Music Making Is Powerful—
Some Diverse Cultural Perspectives

I was fortunate to have grown up in a home where we sang together often—not just in the car, but after meals on Saturday nights and around the campfire in the summertime. We sang great songs—folk songs like "I've Been Working on the Railroad," "Frerè Jacques," and "Swing Low, Sweet Chariot." I still love these songs. To this day, they still help to define who I am; they are part of my personal cultural heritage. Some would argue that "Swing Low, Sweet Chariot" comes from a different heritage than my own Anglo-Saxon roots. It does—it is an African American spiritual. But my family sang it, and we loved singing it; it became part of our lives, even though its true meaning may not have been apparent to all of us.

Over time, that meaning has become apparent to me. Now when I sing "Swing Low, Sweet Chariot," I embrace its anger and joy, its passion and compassion. It is not a song of slavery. It is a song of freedom. The words "Coming for to carry me home" say "Coming to deliver freedom." I keep in mind that when the slaves sang about freedom, they often meant the freedom of death and heaven as well as the freedom from slavery. Songs such as "Swing Low, Sweet Chariot" are not generic songs. They are songs of great power.

In 1983 I moved from Boston to Chicago. Because of my involvement with the Chicago Children's Choir, I became familiar with both black gospel music and the great diverse music from Jewish traditions. I fell in love with both. I fell in love with the cantor's voice with its enormous emotional impact. I fell in love with the gospel preacher's voice—exploding into song—everyone on their feet shouting their praises, nothing held back.

When I went on to pursue a graduate degree, I continued examining the many musical traditions from around the world. They fascinated me. Again, I asked, "Why is music making a powerful experience?" What I learned transported me into a state of awe and wonder—a state of being I hope never to leave. The ways of making music on this planet are astonishingly different in every culture. One of the joyful shocks that hit me was that in many cultures, music is neither entertainment nor art. It is much more. Music is a *living presence* people cannot live without. Music is alive with a power that shapes and changes us.

As I describe some of these musical traditions, my descriptions will be those of an enthusiastic teacher, not an ethnomusicological scholar. Although I have studied and shared in the music of many nations, I do not claim to be an expert on any of these traditions or cultures. The generalities I use are intended to help explain the incredible power I have felt from studying the world's music as well as the power I have experienced during many years of singing, dancing, and sharing this music with students of all ages.

Musical Traditions

Africa is a continent of amazing diversity. In West Africa, for example, there are thousands of different cultures, each with their own musical traditions. Music is present everywhere in all of these cultures, in many different styles.

The music is accompanied by movement—when you sing, you dance. There is seldom a separation of audience and performer—everyone is involved in some way, whether through singing, playing, shouting responses, or dancing. There is no such thing as an untalented person. Everyone can make music. It's part of being alive.

The act of making music is a compassionate act—there is a constant generosity of spirit on the part of those who make music. In most traditional West African cultures, work is accompanied by music. Farmers traditionally have musicians playing as crops are planted or harvested. The music is believed to energize the plants, ensuring that the garden will grow and that the crops will be plentiful. Cooking is accompanied by singing; you sing as you cook—otherwise the food will not come out right. Likewise, shop and factory workers sing to ensure a well-made product. In West Africa, music is not a form of entertainment or amusement or enlightenment. Music is an essential and integral part of the flow of life.

The musicians of Zimbabwe who play mbiras (thumb pianos) are not playing solos on their instruments. They are playing duets—duets with living spirits, the spirits of their ancestors. Ancestors play an important part of the belief system of many African cultures. The spirits sometimes inhabit material objects like thumb pianos, and the music itself becomes almost like the voice of the ancestors. For the Zimbabwe musicians, their music has a living presence.

African cultures are not alone in thinking of music as a living presence and as an integral part of life. In chapter 6, I will show you how to teach the South African song "Thula Klizeo" by Joseph Shabalala. I have taught the song to thousands of children and every time I revel at how the children embrace the song's living tradition and it's energy. I see in the children an African spirit—they are lifted by the living music and made more alive.

There is a Hindu concept called Nada Brahma, which means that the world is made of sound. As part of this Hindu philosophy, sound or vibration is a sacred element present in all things from the vibration of the atom to the resonance of the stars. Life and consciousness are manifestations of sound. A person seeking enlightened consciousness may seek Nada Brahma, a state of being in which one is in harmony with the resonant patterns of the all things. One reaches Nada Brahma through making music.

I once did a Hindu music unit with sixth graders. As part of this, we learned a raga (kind of scale) from India. The students took turns improvising on the raga's melody. During one class, I asked everyone to close their eyes as we sang. The entire session was spent chanting and improvising the song we had learned. We did not attain the Nada Brahma state of consciousness, but there was a general feeling of joyful ecstasy at the end—one where the concept of a living resonant world made a little more sense.

Aboriginal cultures in Australia believe that all things were created by great gods that came out of the earth and sang the world into being. Each god walked what is called a songline; as the god walked, their song created rock formations, plants, animals, and human beings. Aboriginal elders re-create the songlines to ensure that the world will continue to exist. They walk the same invisible paths that the gods walked, and they sing the same songs that have been passed down from generation to generation. To the Aboriginal people of Australia, without music, the world would cease to exist.

There is a Native American expression that I am very fond of, "Walk in Beauty." Variations of this can be found in Hopi and Navajo prayers such as:

> Now I walk in beauty.
> Beauty is before me.
> Beauty is behind me,
> Above and below me.
> Your world is so beautiful.

At first, I assumed that the word *beauty* meant something similar to Plato's concept of beauty—an aesthetic ideal such as a beautiful painting or a beautiful face. By making this assumption, I was applying my own cultural perspective to a perspective I knew little about. I was making a false assumption. This is a very common mistake, one we have to be constantly aware of.

What I have come to understand is that the Navaho concept of beauty relates to a world that is in complete harmony—there is a harmony between air and tree, tree and earth, earth and water. All of these elements are interdependent on each other. Everything is in harmony with everything else. And our purpose as human beings is to live in harmony with the world, not as superiors, but as equals in the circle of life. To walk in beauty means to walk in harmony with creation.

The circle is a constant symbol in most Native American art and ritual. The circle in the sand paintings, in the prayer wheels, and in the dance formations are deliberate reflections of the way many of them see the world— all things are part of a circle. The air, earth, fire, water, and life are present in the circle—all equal interdependent participants—all part of the cycle of events that makes up life.

Most Native American drums have a circular shape and for some Native Americans, the rhythms themselves have circular patterns. An eight-beat pattern, for example, can begin softly, getting louder on every beat and ending with a loud downbeat, then starting again softly. This pattern of constantly going toward the next beat, as opposed to away from the previous beat, is one of many ways that the mind-set behind the music manifests itself in the music. The drum rhythm is moving like a wheel.

Like the mbiras of Zimbabwe, many Native American drums are thought to have a living presence. When the animal is killed, a prayer is made to honor the animal as an equal. The prayer asks that the spirit of the animal be present in the skin of the drum. It is hoped that when such a drum is played, the spirit of the animal will enter the drummer. The sound and the music are thought to be alive.

There is a Navaho word, *hózhóó* [ho-jeau, soft "j" as in the French *bonjour*]. It refers to the importance of space. One might say that a certain space is beautiful. The term *beauty*, remember, refers to all things being in harmony with each other. Hózhóó, then, refers to a space that is in harmony. When you make music, you must think of the space around you as being in harmony—a part of the circle.

I discussed the Native American concept of beauty and hózhóó during a singing celebration once. It began to rain outside during our last song. As we softly hummed the last chord, we heard thunder outside. There was lightning. An Apache friend, Ernestine Cody, was there. As we stood and listened to the rain and thunder, she remarked that her people had many names for rain. The rain that is accompanied by thunder and lightning, she said, was a male rain. "The male ancestors, with tears in their eyes, are here to hold us—to be with us." At that moment everyone in the room understood and deeply felt the power of hózhóó. We could feel our part in the harmony of all things. We walked in beauty.

Among some Native Americans, when a person becomes ill—whether mentally, physically, or spiritually—it means that they are no longer in harmony with the world. To be healed, that person can return to nature and re-absorb nature's harmony. They are healed by listening to the harmony with more than their ears—they listen with body, mind, and spirit. Some call this journey of recovery a vision quest.

The healing power of music is used in many cultures. Music healing rituals almost always include singing and dancing. Through these rituals, people achieve trance states in which truly amazing transformations can take place. Though the effect of music healing is the same, various cultures have adapted unique perspectives. For example, healers in the mountains of India form diagnoses based on the voice of an ill person. Some Native American healers use similar techniques.

When I first heard of the connection between music and healing, I was very skeptical. How could you hear that a person was ill? I have since come to realize that my ears have become deadened by our noisy modern world. My ancestors heard things I do not. Modern day sound healers are sensitive to resonance or sound at all levels.

Later in this chapter, I will briefly discuss chakras, the Eastern concept of tunings within the body. Modern day sound healers see the chakra points as our body's harmonic system—our way of being in harmony with ourselves—body, mind, and spirit.

In ancient China almost all aspects of their culture were based on the five notes of their pentatonic scale—five notes representing the five elements of earth, air, water, fire, and metal. Distances were based on the length of a wooden flute. Volume was based on the number of seeds that could be placed inside the flute. All flutes were tuned to a bell in the emperor's possession. People lived in harmony with others in the same way that musical notes live in harmony. One's place in society was often based on how well one listened, on how educated one's ear was. Educated people could listen to the wind or to another person's voice and discover things as if they were reading a book. A wise person, or a sage, was one who listened well. Compare this with the

.estern concept of a wise person as someone with vision—two different cultures, one with perspectives based on listening, the other based on seeing.

There is validity to the phrase "Music calms the savage beast." Music is used universally to calm people. Lullabies the world over calm children to sleep. Teachers of younger students know the effect a calm song can have on the children. I knew a kindergarten teacher who could almost hypnotize her students with a soft slow song. When she started to sing in her calm steady voice, the children would immediately focus their attention on her, no matter how hectic the classroom may have been a moment before.

In almost every world religion, some form of chant is sung to raise the spiritual consciousness of the worshipers. The constant repetition of the melodies and rhythms helps to create trancelike states of consciousness. Even the simple ritual of singing a hymn in a place of worship induces a slightly altered state of mind; the worshiper enters a sacred time and space, and the powers of the music take over.

Music is also used everywhere to rouse people. We want to dance when we hear upbeat music. Marching music and fanfares of all kinds tend to lift our spirits. The sound of the drums and bagpipes of Scotland were meant to do more than rouse people, the sounds were intended to scare their enemies into running away.

There is nothing silly or old-fashioned about having children march to a steady uplifting beat. It is the most natural thing in the world. Repetitive chant is good too.

There are fascinating patterns in the music of the world's cultures—patterns showing that music is a living force, a force that affects us in many ways—inspiring us, healing us, calming us, and uniting us as communities.

The New Views on the Power of Music

Research in many scientific fields is now beginning to reveal what many cultures have believed for a long time. This research is leading to a vision of music as a living presence, a power that sits at the center of life itself (Berendt 1983, 119). This vision, however, is based on many different theories, and scientists are always quick to point out that theories are not facts. Therefore, the vision I now propose is theoretical, not factual. At the least, it makes for an exciting metaphor—a new and refreshing perspective from which to view the world. My purpose in presenting this theory is to stress how extremely important music is for education, far more important than realized ever before.

The term *new paradigm* refers to a way of thinking about ourselves and the world around us that has evolved from traditional worldviews. For example, we once viewed all actions as being independent, machinelike events. We now see that all actions self-organize within interdependent systems. For example, the old view saw the human body as an elaborate machine with each part serving its own function. The lungs processed air, the heart pumped blood, the ears heard sound, the voice made sound. Every action was seen as a separate, independent action. The new view sees the human body as one interdependent living system in which the heart is involved with the lungs' processing of air, and the lungs are involved with the heart's pumping of blood, and so on. Every part of the body is involved with every other part. We need to listen in order to sing—the ear and the voice are interconnected parts of the same process. The actions of the ear affect the body and brain. The old view saw the activities of the brain and the rest of the body as being separate. New paradigm thinkers think of body and mind as part of a whole living system. Consciousness itself is not seen as a separate entity. The whole body is conscious.

Along these lines, the practitioners of holistic health have become very aware that the brain plays an integral part in healing. According to the old view, if an organ was diseased, the standard approach was to think of the body as a machine—you fixed the broken part. Now, we see the whole body is involved with healing itself. The brain and body, working in harmony, are capable of great wonders. And, from our new perspective, the miracles brought about by ancient shamans, who used chant, dance, and trance to heal, no longer seem primitive.

Interdependence

An interdependent system is one in which every action affects every other action. A forest fire in Brazil affects the weather in Moscow by creating huge dust clouds that eventually float over Russia. Every element in an ecosystem depends on every other element, even the so-called nonliving elements such as minerals, oxygen, and sunlight. Yes, light is an integral element of all life. The sun is food for many of earth's life forms. Physicists speak of photons of light as being interchangeable. When the light from an object hits a person, only some of it bounces off. Most of the photons are absorbed into the person. Its energy becomes that person's energy. This is how incredible interdependence is—everything is constantly becoming everything else—as when you spend a lot of time in a forest or at a beach. More than memory remains with you after you have left.

After a powerful singing celebration, I leave with the power of the event still with me. The sense of harmony and connectedness remains. This feeling of being connected to everything is an incredible feeling—truly transcending. We walk in beauty, in harmony with the world around us.

The meanings of the survival of the fittest do not work in the context of an interdependent system. A herd of caribou, for example, survive by caring for each other, protecting each other from harm. And yes, the wolf survives by attacking the caribou, but the wolf attacks the weakest member of the herd, thus ensuring the strength of the herd as a whole. The survival instinct is universal. Competition and cooperation are both parts of this instinct.

When we sing together, our cooperation and interdependence become the perfect analogy for the interdependence and cooperation within nature.

Children singing together are learning how to cooperate—literally how to live in harmony with one another.

Although we humans claim that it is independence from each other that we crave, we truly cannot live without each other or other forms of living things. All life is interdependent with all other life. We have many kinds of bacteria that live inside our bodies. Without them, we could not digest our food. The bacteria are not separate guests inside us—they are part of us, what biologists call host/parasite relationships. We aren't as independent as we think. This also applies to our place in both our cultures and the natural world. We are very interdependent creatures.

Part of what makes interdependent systems work is the fact that there is such amazing diversity in the world—not one kind of flower, but thousands, each different, each helping the ecosystem in its own way.

It is no coincidence that each person is different. Like the world we live in, diversity is part of our character. Our diversity makes us strong (Sahtouris 1989, 27). A classroom of children is full of amazing diversity—different races, religions, economic groups—different learning styles, abilities, and interests. The diversity of each classroom is like the diversity in all of nature. It is natural. There is a combined strength that can be drawn from the diversity.

There is a culture in West Africa that has a traditional dance in which the dancers dance to a beat that none of the drummers are playing. This beat is called the God-beat. The many different rhythmic patterns sound chaotic to the uninitiated ear. They sound like independent beats. In actuality, each rhythmic pattern is interdependent with every other pattern. The resulting rhythmic texture is based entirely on the inaudible God-beat. And it is the dancers that create the God-beat. It is their part in this process to dance to the beat that no one is playing. There is an interdependence between drummers and dancers.

Once we have gained an understanding of what the new paradigm is all about, including the concepts of holism and interdependence, then we are ready to ask the big question—How does the universe work? Answer: The universe and the music it is made of are self-organized living systems (Swimme 1984, 127–39; Sahtouris 1989, 19–20). I could say that it is an amazing, mysterious, and magnificent self-organized system, but words cannot quite describe the awe and wonder I feel when thinking about this. I am even more awe inspired when I think of the billions of years of evolution needed in order for this thought to occur.

The Harmony of Things

If the universe consisted of only one atom, there wouldn't be much for that atom to do. It would have no other atoms to react with—it would have no one to play with. The atom would be in a perfectly balanced state—in total harmony with itself. There would be no need for evolution—perfection would already have been reached. There would be no change. But because the world contains many atoms, there is a constant interaction between the atoms, creating constant change and constant evolution. Just as a single atom would be in a state of complete balance, so many atoms together strive for balance. For example, an oxygen atom needs eight electrons in its outer shell to be balanced, but it only has six. To achieve the balance it needs, it may, under the right conditions, attach itself to two hydrogen atoms that provide the necessary two electrons—H_2O. Thus, balance is created, and water is formed.

The balance created by atoms and molecules can be said to be a harmony. The resonances of each atom are in harmony with each other. In nature, there is a constant striving for this harmony—the balance of all parts.

When you press the sustain pedal (the right pedal) on a piano and play a single note, you can actually hear other notes ringing if you listen carefully. These higher notes are called harmonics. Harmonics occur any time an acoustic sound is created. Harmonics ring very softly. Every voice and instrument creates many harmonics. If a flute and a violin both played the same note, each would create harmonics that we would hear as timbre or tone color. Take away these harmonics, and the violin and the flute would both sound the same.

You can create harmonics on a stringed instrument such as a guitar by touching your finger tip lightly on the string exactly half way down the neck of the guitar (the lower or thicker strings work best). While holding your finger at the halfway point (without pressing down too hard), pluck the string. The soft note you hear is that string's first and lowest harmonic. It sounds an octave, or eight notes, above the whole string's pitch.

You can find harmonics on a recorder simply by the way you exhale. Without covering any of the holes, blow softly and steadily into the mouthpiece. You will hear a quiet note. Now blow harder. The note will suddenly jump up an octave, or eight notes. That note, again, is the first and lowest harmonic.

Notice that in the case of the guitar and the recorder, the first and lowest harmonic was an octave higher than the original note. This is because all harmonics follow the same simple mathematical rules, the rules being based on simple ratios. It's as simple as one, two, three, four. The first and lowest harmonic sounds at the ratio of one to two or 1/2. On a guitar, that would be half the length of the string. The next, second to lowest harmonic, would sound at the ratio of two to three, two thirds the length of the string. Similarly, the following harmonics follow the same pattern: 3/4ths and 4/5ths. You can easily figure out the next harmonics simply by continuing the pattern of adding to both the top and bottom numbers, 5/6ths, 6/7ths, and so forth. The higher the numbers, the higher the pitches.

C^1	1:2
G^1	2:3
C^2	3:4
E^2	4:5
G^2	5:6

In terms of music, these harmonics form the basis for our scales and chords. When the first five harmonics are sounded simultaneously, they form what is called a major chord, consisting of the first, third, and fifth notes in the scale. When all the harmonics are spelled out and reordered, you have the basis for our major scale (with a raised or higher fourth, which is probably how many ancient civilizations heard their scales). If the note C was the fundamental (the key we are in—the lowest note of the scale) then the overtones (in order) would be C, C^1, G^1, C^2, E^2, G^2, $B\flat^2$, C^3, D^3, E^3, $F\sharp^3$, G^3, A^3, and so forth. If you spelled them out in their scale sequence, without the repetitions, you would have $C, D, E, F\sharp, G, A, B\flat, C$.

✪   ✪

There is a fun science/math project you can do with your students. You will need a saw for cutting metal, lubricant for the saw, a ruler, some foam rubber, a metal file, some metal pipe, and an awl for marking the pipe. Ask for ½-inch-thin wall conduit pipe, otherwise known as EMT (Electro-Metallic Tubing.) You can build your own xylophone by cutting the pipe according to the ratios mentioned a moment ago. Using the metric system, cut five identical lengths about thirty-six cm long according to the following ratios: 1/1, 1/2, 1/3, 1/4, 1/5 and 2/3, 3/4, and 4/5. (Note: the 1/3 and 2/3 would be cut from one piece, the 1/4 and 3/4 from another, etc.) File off the ends of the pipes so no one gets cut. Place the pipes on the foam rubber in order by height. Voila! You have a tuned xylophone. It's a great activity for learning ratios.

Notice that in the overtone series listed a moment ago, both *C* and *G* appear three times. These two notes can be looked at as being the grand pillars that hold harmony and music together. The interval (distance) between these two notes is a fifth. In Western music theory this interval is called a perfect fifth. Hundreds of years ago, the perfect fifth was considered a sacred interval, an interval of great importance in music. The solfège names that form the major scale—do, re, mi, fa, sol, la, ti, do—have Latin roots; do and sol (the first and fifth) are the most important. The word *do* comes from *Domine*, the word for God; and *sol* comes from the word *solar*, the word for sun.

European cultures are not the only ones to place importance on the interval of the fifth. Ancient Egyptians and early Greeks, including the mathematician Pythagorus, knew of the importance of the fifth. Remember that the octave has a ratio of one to two and that the fifth has a ratio of two to three. Buildings like the Parthenon were built with these ratios in mind. Both the cultures of India and China referred to the fifth as being of sacred importance (McClellan 1991, 120–30). Five notes in the Chinese scale, for example, correspond with their five elements of the universe.

In most cultures of the world the intonation or tuning of the scale notes changes, but the fifth remains the same. The second, third, fourth, sixth, and seventh notes of the scale can be sung flat, sharp (lower, higher), or not at all, but the first and fifth notes remain the same. It should be noted that to American listeners, these notes sound peculiar or off, but to many cultures, these flat or sharp notes sound normal. The pitches in the scale are relative. The major scale in the Western world has subtle differences in its tunings depending on the style and period of the music. The mbira players of Zimbabwe don't tune their instruments, they chune them, which is to say that every mbira ensemble has its own unique way of tuning the pitches of the scale. In India, there are formalized scale tunings called ragas. There are over eight hundred different ragas, an amazingly diverse number of ascending and descending scale possibilities.

Resonant points in the human body, the parts of the body that are affected by external and internal sounds, are called chakras. Many specialists within the holistic health movement refer to the Eastern concept of chakras (Gardner 1990, 1–3). You and your students can easily understand the concept by singing resonant oh-shaped vowels on a low note. Feel in your body where that sound vibrates. It will be different for everybody, but the stomach or chest area is usually where you will feel the sound. Now try a higher ah-shaped vowel. The sound may vibrate in the chest or neck area. Try a higher eh-shaped vowel, then a very high ee-shaped vowel. These will probably vibrate in the lower and upper parts of the head, respectively. Experiment with these vowel sounds. Sing them higher and lower to feel the changes in vibration. Sing them with more resonance by making the sound more nasal. This will probably increase the vibrations.

I feel that there is a great deal of wisdom in the Eastern notion of chakras, although I am not ready to accept all the information surrounding them. For our purposes, we need to understand that the whole body, not just the ears, responds to resonance. Furthermore, we need only to understand that different organs of the body have their own subtle rhythms and vibrations. In other words, we resonate. This is a magnificent idea.

Entrainment

Resonance, technically speaking, refers to sound waves. There are different kinds of sound waves with differing shapes, some smooth, some rough. The pitch of a sound wave can be determined by the number of vibrations per second. For example, a sound that vibrates 440 times per second would create the pitch A. As with harmonics, simple ratios can be used to find other notes. For example, half of 440 is 220. This pitch would sound an octave lower: What vibrates? In the case of the piano, the strings vibrate. The A would vibrate 440 times per second making the air vibrate at the same frequency.

These vibrations are very fast pulses or beats. We could say that since the pitch A is a vibration of 440 cycles per second—it therefore has a pulse of 440 beats per second—that is the speed of its rhythm. I am using the word *rhythm* loosely—for our purposes, a rhythm is any kind of steady pulse. We can say that all vibrations are ultimately made up of beats or rhythms, although most of the time, these rhythms are going so fast, we do not hear them as rhythms. It is important, nonetheless, to understand pitches as being rhythms or pulses, because there is an amazing element to rhythm called entrainment that is essential to our story.

Entrainment is a phenomenon of nature where one rhythm copies another rhythm. Entrainment happens at many levels of nature, from the atomic level to the level of human behavior. It is certainly part of our response to music.

Two people walking down the street will eventually step to the same beat. They entrain. Audiences listening to music will tap their toes to the same beat, and often, without knowing it, they will breathe to the same beat. Some Native American groups entrain their heartbeats with the drum beats—they make the rhythm of the their heart and the drum the same.

When a car mechanic tunes an engine, all parts of the machine must entrain with each other in order for there to be a smooth running engine. Tuning a piano is similar to tuning an engine. You must make the strings entrain with each other. On the piano, A is actually three strings. All three strings must vibrate 440 times per second. They must have the same rhythm.

When a group of people sing in tune with each other, they are entraining. When there are some singing out of tune, however, the sound is muddy and the effect is like driving an untuned car. When everyone is singing in tune, on the other hand, there is a ringing magical quality to the sound. In fact, it goes beyond this. We are like the two tuning forks just mentioned. When we sing, we entrain with each other in a most powerful way. Our singing together is as automatic as the second tuning fork matching the resonance of the first.

Crystal glasses can be cracked through entrainment. When you tap a crystal glass, you will hear a ringing pitch. If you can accurately re-create that pitch loud enough, you will make the glass vibrate or entrain with that pitch, which, remember, is a fast rhythm. If the vibration is more than the glass's structure can withstand, it will shatter. Sometimes a radio will be playing music and a lamp or some other object in the room will begin to vibrate. This is called "sympathetic vibrations." The lamp is entraining with a pitch being played in the music.

you sang—certain strings of the piano will entrain to your voice creating sympathetic vibrations. This is a fun activity to do with children.

✪ ✪

Biologists know that if you remove the beating hearts from two frogs, they will have two separate rhythms until you place them near each other. Then they will entrain with each other and their heartbeats will be identical.

We dance in entrainment. The adrenaline of early human beings would pump them up when they heard loud sounds. The adrenaline rush would give them extra strength for running away or for protecting themselves. When these loud sounds were accompanied by rhythms as with drumming, the adrenaline began pumping, but instead or running away, people entrained with the rhythm and danced.

We are entraining with each other's speech patterns all the time. I learned this the hard way when I first taught kindergarten. I could not understand why students were crawling under tables and why, no matter how much I talked, they simply didn't seem to hear what I said. I later realized that by talking in a fast agitated voice, they entrained with the rhythm of my speech and became hyperactive. Talking slowly in a calm voice settled the students down. Different songs created different moods with the students. This, of course, works with people of all ages. A fast song will lift our spirits. A slow song will calm the savage beast in us. This is largely due to entrainment.

Muzak and now New Age music capitalizes on the effect of entrainment on us. There is nothing wrong with music that purposely removes the stress from our lives. Some New Age composers like Don Campbell are very aware of how we react to rhythms. Some of his rhythms can only be perceived on a subconscious level. Understanding the many rhythms of the body, he composes music with similar rhythms. His music can simultaneously affect the brain waves and the subtle rhythms of the body's organs. Understanding these rhythms makes music a powerful tool for affecting the body and mind.

The ancient Buddhists rang a matching pair of small bells called prayer bells. The sound of the bells would induce an almost instantaneous meditative state of mind. We now know why. This is another of the many ways in which ancient wisdom and modern science join together. Our brain emits brain waves. When there are between thirteen and thirty brain waves per second our minds are in a very awake and active state (Beta). When there are six or seven brain waves per second, we are in a meditative state. The prayer bells, when rung, create a subtle rhythm of six or seven beats per second. It is believed that our brain waves then entrain with that rhythm, creating a meditative state (Gardner 1990, 77).

I can go into an auditorium full of highly vocal children and ring my Tibetan prayer bell. There will be immediate silence. The bell has a powerful trance-inducing quality that children react to instantaneously.

Education researchers have recently been discussing the rhythms of learning (Brewer and Campbell 1991, 89–144). The rhythm of a child's day becomes a familiar rhythm after a while, a rhythm that most teachers understand shouldn't be tinkered with too much. Children need that sense of rhythm from hour to hour (Brewer and Campbell 1991, 26–36). There's more to this. For example, children aged two to six do much of their learning through body movement. Rhythmic movement can be used to aid memory, increase pattern awareness, aid listening abilities, and increase attention spans (Brewer and Campbell 1991, 147–53). The many rhythms of the body are affected constantly by entrainment, and these rhythms ultimately affect the rhythms of learning.

Many elementary school teachers now play music in the background during study times. A lot of research has gone into the use of background music for accelerated learning. Many experts recommend Baroque instrumental music, others Gregorian chant or New Age music (Campbell 1992, 65; Brewer and Campbell 1991, 253–57). It is up to each teacher to decide what music works best.

Self-Organized Systems

But why do rhythms copy each other? What makes harmonics ring out according to simple ratios? What makes the oxygen molecule join with the two hydrogen atoms? Is there a mysterious force controlling these actions? Were these actions planned long ago? Are they chance happenings? What makes these things happen? The answer is so simple it seems totally obvious, and yet it is a relatively new concept among scientists. The answer is that these actions are self-organized (Swimme 1984, 127–39).

Both the H_2O chemical reaction and the harmonic overtones self-organize according to mathematical formulas. They create a balance.

In the case of the water molecule, the oxygen and hydrogen molecules created a simple balance of electrons—they self-organized in a way that can be explained mathematically. In the case of the harmonic overtone system, the overtones self-organized automatically in a way that can be explained through simple ratios. Not all self-organized systems can be explained so easily. In fact, we do not know how most actions self-organize. The complicating factor is that everything is interdependent, which means that any single action must be self-organized both within itself as well as with the entire living system. To understand any single event, we must also understand its relationship with the world around it.

The best example of a vast interdependent self-organized system is the earth itself. The term *Gaia Hypotheses* is used to explain this phenomenon (Sahtouris 1989, 19–26). Our atmosphere contains oxygen, hydrogen, carbon, and other molecules. This was not always so. When life was beginning on this planet, the atmosphere was hydrogen, carbon, sulfur, and other elements— an unbreathable mix for us, but we weren't here yet. The early life-forms, leading up to bacteria, evolved over an enormous amount of time—three quarters of the time that there has been life on this planet (Swimme and Berry.

1992, 97–111; Sahtouris 1989, 50–84). In gradual stages, bacteria learned to eat three things: the minerals of the earth (including other bacteria), the carbon and selected elements in the atmosphere, and the energy of the sun. They could not, however, digest oxygen, so the oxygen molecules were sent into the atmosphere. Thanks to the bacteria, we now have an atmosphere with oxygen in it—a breathable atmosphere.

The amazing thing is that the bacteria created just the right amount of oxygen in the atmosphere. Even one percentage more or less would be harmful to the earth. Until the pollutants of recent years, the earth was able to keep a constant and healthy balance in its atmosphere. If the airborne cloud from a volcano or asteroid explosion darkened the skies, an imbalance would be created. The bacteria would then compensate, recreating the balance. The atmosphere, in conjunction with the bacteria, the oceans, the earth, and the sun, self-organized. Even volcanoes and asteroids were necessary for the balance, as they provided a constant supply of new elements to the atmosphere, water, and soil of the earth. From this viewpoint, the earth is seen as one complete living system. The earth is not a planet with life on it; it is a living planet.

The solar system we are a part of is also a living system, as it is essential to the self-organizing patterns of the living system we call life. We can say the same of the Milky Way galaxy and indeed, of the entire universe. The new story of our universe is unfolding to reveal that long before the first DNA cells were formed, the universe was one vast self-organizing system (Sahtouris 1989, 68–71).

All self-organizing systems seem to be part of a greater system. The indigenous people who see the world as being alive are very wise. We have come to see that the Native American belief that all things are in harmony is a reality. This harmony is the result of a world where all actions are interdependent. There interdependent actions strive for a balance like the oxygen atom needing hydrogen in order to be balanced. The oxygen and hydrogen form a harmony. Self-organizing systems are systems in harmony with themselves and with the world around them (Swimme and Berry 1992, 22–29). We see the Hindu philosophy of Nada Brahma, that the world is made of sound, as also being relevant to our story, because at the heart of this amazing living system called the universe is resonance—the resonance of every atom and every being.

This chapter embraces a new paradigm in science, the New Story, and its relevance to the powers of music. I have proposed that this new model be used in shaping both the multicultural and multiple intelligences perspectives in education and particularly the role of music in education.

The old view of the earth is that of a planet with life on it. Our old view of music is that of human-made sounds added to entertain or enlighten us. The new view of the earth is one of a living planet. The new view of music is one of a living harmonious force within the universe itself. The universe is drawn toward harmony in the same way we are. Music is a force far more powerful than we have ever realized—a power that every culture on the planet has hinted at in amazing ways. Now, due to the sharing of cultural practices, these powers are coming together, and we are receiving a hint of the magnificent possibilities.

As I said at the beginning of this chapter, this was written to explain to my mind what my heart already knew.

When we are in groups and we are singing in joyful harmony, we can feel all the things written about in this chapter—we can feel the living force of music. We can feel a sense of interdependence with the world around us. We become a part of the living harmony.

The Story of Music

· · · · · · · · · · · · · · · · · · · THE PREVIOUS chapter discussed different perspectives on the powers of music, and it explained the importance of sound and music in the evolution of the universe. Now we will look at the role of music in the story of human evolution. What is the connection between the evolution of music and the evolution of humanity? Recently developed research fields, such as evolutionary psychology, provide exciting new theories showing that music and humanity could not have evolved without the other (Menuhin and Davis 1979, 1–43; Campbell 1989, 86).

Some of My Best Friends Are Mammals

We begin our story with the mammals. If the evolution of the known universe were to fit into a single day, mammals would not appear until the last few seconds—a fascinating few seconds, to say the least.

Mammals evolved on land and sea from earlier reptiles. Mammals retained all the evolutionary advances of the reptiles, including the senses— seeing, hearing, feeling, smelling, and tasting.

The ability to hear and produce sounds is significant. These sounds— ranging from the small vibrations of the queen ant pounding her body on the ground to the loud cry of the wolf—are forms of communication; they are languages. And these sound languages are diverse. Elephants hear sub-frequencies that are too low for humans to hear, and dogs hear sounds that are too high. Birds sing an amazing repertoire of songs, often imitating and augmenting each other's melodies. Whales send their long, slow melodies through highly conductive water. In fact, before the age of noisy motorized ocean vessels, whales could communicate across great oceans. Without sound, nature's diverse rituals of reproduction would have been impossible. Our reptilian and mammalian ancestors would have become extinct long ago if they could not have communicated through sound production and listening.

It is an astounding revelation that every life-form that can make sounds, does.

The cochlea is the part of the ear that hears. Our ears reach out to the world around us. We reach out with our ears as well as our voices. For our ancestors, reaching out with their ears was their best protection from danger.

The ear controls hearing and balance. Mammals feel balanced on all four legs due to the balancing mechanism of the two semicircular canals above the cochlea, perpendicular to each other. The canals help balance in much the same way that a carpenter's level tool determines horizontal surfaces.

The mammalian brain, which developed on top of the reptilian brain, was a major evolutionary step, which added elements of emotion. For the first time, bonds were created between mother and offspring. Reptiles lay their eggs, then go on with their lives. Reptiles, on the whole, have no relationship with their offspring. Mammals, such as bears and apes, on the other hand, began not only to care for their young, but they also began to do something quite radical—they began to teach their young. Baby mammals became very dependent on the grown-ups, learning from them through imitation and play (Dissanayake 1990, 4–25). And a new physical dexterity increased their ability to play with each other. We've all seen images of bear cubs rolling around and interacting with their elders in playful ways. We've also seen images of mother apes holding their infants in their arms, nurturing and protecting them.

A Mother Holds Her Young and Sings Her Gratitude

Imagine a proud mother primate, lovingly holding her child. Like other living creatures, she communicates using sounds. She has learned that simple sounds affect her child. She makes an *oo* sound. The sound calms the child. Suddenly, a predator comes near. The mother signals a warning by repeating a high *ee* sound. These sounds are simply the vocalization of the emotions felt by the mother. The sounds became the basic vowel sounds common in most languages—the surprised *oh!*, the calming *oo*, the wondrous *ah!*

Anthropologists now believe that early humans sang or chanted long before they spoke. This theory is based on the anatomy of the jaw and face bones of early humans. So, what was the nature of the songs they sang or chanted? They were the expressions of mammalian emotions. It happens that, as the early humans evolved, these sounds became the bases for languages.

With the exception of the mothers' lullabies, it is likely that dance accompanied the chanting. You will remember that the previous chapter referred to the origins of dance as a natural reaction to loud repeated rhythms. The brain sent adrenaline through the body, but instead of running away or protecting itself, the early human entrained with the beat and danced.

Just as the mammalian brain had grown on top of the reptilian brain, the new human brain, the cortex, grew over the reptilian and mammalian brains. As a result, we humans now have what is called a triune brain, three interdependent brains. The neocortex is our language- and symbol-processing area. Thinking occurs in all three brains, but the neocortex has the difficult, and sometimes seemingly impossible, task of putting everything together.

Some important changes happened in these early stages of human evolution. Previously, mammals had been born with fairly mature brains and bodies—much like newborn horses that are off and running within hours of their birth. Our ape ancestors were probably like that, but over a long period of time, infants were born with increasingly less developed brains and bodies. This meant that more and more behavioral learning had to take place after birth. The child learned through emotional dialogue with its mother and through playful interaction with the world around it. The important evolutionary point is that the brain continued to develop after birth. This is part of the reason why the third part of the human brain, the cortex, developed.

Another reason may be due to the change that occurred in the ear of the early human. The most important function of the ear is to balance the body. The ear of our reptile ancestors had one canal that allowed them to be on all fours with their bellies to the earth. If they tipped over for some reason, their ears became disoriented. Our mammalian ancestors had two canals in the ear, which gave them better balance. With the development of the third semicircular canal, the early human was able to balance herself on two legs. Don Campbell, a specialist on music and the brain, suggests that our becoming vertical allowed the cortex to develop (Campbell 1989, 86). In other words, our advanced brain could not have evolved without the change in the ear.

I have suggested three of many reasons for the evolution of the human brain. First, the strong emotional bond between mother and child resulted in early forms of chanted language. The development of this language meant increased memory and symbol-processing ability—we needed bigger brains. Second, infants were increasingly born with underdeveloped brains, allowing the brains to continue developing after birth. This led, over thousands of generations, to an astounding growth in the size of the neocortex. Third, the balance function of the ear assisted humans in becoming vertical, which also allowed a more advanced neocortex to develop.

Note the important role played by sound and listening in the evolution of the brain and in the further development of the ear, which led to increased brain size and the beginnings of language due to the sung chant of the mother-child bond. There is, however, another related reason for the evolution of the human brain, one in which sound and music are of monumental importance.

The Third Function of the Ear

The traditional view of human anatomy emphasizes two purposes of the human ear—balancing the body and hearing sounds. A new theory by Alfred Tomatis is showing, however, that there is a third and extremely important function of the ear—to *charge* the brain—to act like a battery and, in very simple terms, stimulate the actions of the brain whether they be meditative or highly creative. This charging of the brain begins in the womb. Just as the umbilical cord helps feed the fetus's body, the sound of the parents' voices help feed the fetus's brain (Gilmore, Madaule, and Thompson 1989, 7).

At six months in the womb, according to this controversial theory, the fetus is able to hear only the highest frequencies, particularly percussive sounds like *x*, *t*, and *ch*. The phrase "What a pretty baby" might be heard as *T . . . Pr . . . T*; the softer sounds of *wh* and *b* might not be heard. After birth as the child matures, the cochlea gradually hears lower and lower sounds. The brain continues to be stimulated by the sounds.

In the womb, the high sounds of the parent's voices are received in the ears of the fetus. The sounds are like food for the brain, stimulating brain cells to grow and be energized—and helping in the formation of connections among brain cells. Sound, according to this theory, is a kind of brain food (Gilmore 1987, 7). The hunger for sound equates with the hunger for mental stimulation and the hunger for learning. Children who no longer hunger for sound lose their desire to learn (Gilmore 1987, 20–37). Therapists are able to help children with learning problems, even autistic children, by reviving the hunger for sound and mental stimulation.

The environment of early prehumans must have been full of exciting sounds. It is likely that singing and dancing became part of everyday life. This highly charged sound environment must have influenced the evolving human child, whose brain was already growing.

At first, community singing and dancing for humans were not all that different from the play activities of other mammals in that they involved imitation, exaggeration, improvisation, and repetition. If you think about it, the elements of play are the same elements present in music: imitation, exaggeration, improvisation, and repetition. Gradually, what had been play took on a new importance: It became ritual.

Sounds, in the form of words, took on special meanings. Sounds, or vocalized emotions, became language. And just as sounds took on meanings, so did physical objects. Among the remains of early humans, anthropologists have found colorful and specially carved stones. To the early humans, these were objects of great power. These objects had meanings and purpose. Just as tools helped in the labor of the body, these aesthetic artifacts helped in the labor of the mind—connections to mythologies and the stories of existence were aided by the use of these physical symbols, stones, carvings, paintings, and clothes.

The chants and stories that were sung took on the same level of impor-tance. They were essential for the early people to know who they were and what their place in the universe was. And these chants were reinforced by repetition from generation to generation—sung first in small tribes until today in our communities and cultures, our extended TV tribes.

Music, chant, and singing still help to define who we are. They continue to bring us together as cultures. Music still charges the brain. Resonance and rhythm are still at the heart of our being—from the rhythms of our hearts to the resonances of our brain waves, we are musical creatures, shaped by sound. We create music as a response to the music within us. Just as a star cannot help but shine, we cannot help but sing. It has been essential for our development thus far, and it is essential for our ongoing evolution.

A Creation Story for Children
Told from a Musical Perspective

Now I'm going to tell you a story. It is a creation story, one that is based loosely on the creation stories within Native American, Aboriginal, and Hindu mythologies, but is also based on what many now call the "New Story" (Swimme and Berry 1992, 1–5).

You can learn a lot about a culture by studying its story of creation, of how the world was made and of how it works. Such a story helps guide the members of the culture, connecting them in a community, providing them with a moral standard to live by.

But before I begin, here are two hypothetical examples: The members of culture "X" believe that they were created by a loving Mother in the sky who gives birth to all things. This loving Mother is still alive and watching over her children—the trees, the wind, the grasshoppers, and yes, the human beings. In such a culture, the people see themselves as brothers and sisters to all other life-forms and tend to respect all living things. Their lives are centered in nature.

People in culture "Y", on the other hand, believe that they are created by a committee of wise businesspeople who manufacture all things with the intent of making a profit. In such a culture, the people are likely to be greedy and unloving. Each individual life is centered on itself. There is no community. There is certainly no singing. Where's the profit in that?

The creation story I'm going to tell you isn't as farfetched as the two previous stories. My version of the story uses music and harmony as parts of a metaphor. Like all creation stories, mine is metaphorical. Like all creation stories, however, it can teach us quite a lot.

The New Story is partly based on what astronomers call the "Big Bang." It is an unproven theory that suggests that all things in the universe—every star, planet, and tree—were connected billions of years ago in a single event, an explosion that expanded from a central source. It was energy becoming matter, matter becoming life, and life becoming consciousness.

The notion that we were once stars is pretty radical. Five hundred years ago, European cultures heard some equally radical news that changed the way they saw themselves. Columbus had discovered that the earth was round and that there was a great new continent to be "explored." Many refused to believe the new information about the round planet, just as many now refuse to believe the new story of creation. Since it may never be proven, that is perfectly okay. For those who accept the story, however, the change in thinking will be far grander than the change encountered five hundred years ago by the discovery of a new continent. The New Story is not a threat to any of the world religions. Many religions, in fact, are beginning to embrace the story and to incorporate it into their theology (Fox 1983, 15–16).

You may, if you wish, tell this story to your classes using sound effects and/or visuals. For example, when the narrator comes to each asterisk, he or she could pause and a child could ring a beautifully resonant bell. Avoid using a bell that brings connotations of alarms, churches, or school yards. New Age shops and catalogs sell Tibetan prayer bells as well as other kinds of meditative bell sounds. These bells are ideal.

At the point in the story where life begins, another child can begin to beat a quiet heartbeat on a low hand drum. This heartbeat can continue through to the end of the story. Other sounds, such as animal sounds, can be added as you wish. At the end, everyone can stand and sing a rousing song of your choosing—something like "This Little Light of Mine." Even better, everyone can sing and dance around the room. The story can be performed as a short skit. If performed, the audience can be involved in the singing and dancing at the end. They can even be involved in the middle, making *ooh* and *ah* sounds at the appropriate times.

Before beginning the story, you will want to make it clear to the students that this is only a story. It is not a religious belief, and the story is not intended to alter anyone's religious beliefs. Most religions have their own versions of how the world began, and it is important for us to honor and respect each of those versions.

A CREATION STORY FOR CHILDREN

Once upon a time and space, there was no time nor space.
No music, sound, nor elephants, there was no human race.
    There was no light. There was no dark.
    No planets, stars, nor bears,
There wasn't even nothing, no here, no anyplace.

And this ... Is where ... Our story begins:

In the beginning ... was the big bell.*
    The sound of the bell was amazing and full.
    It was made of all the sounds that were yet to be.

It was made of stars that were to be you and me.

This sound,* that was all there was, spread through space,
filling it with light and energy. It is as if the sound were alive as it
traveled in every direction at once.

The sound kept growing and growing
        just like a living thing,
but there was no one there to hear
        this sound's amazing ring.*

        Or at least, not yet.

This living sound, this energy, it grew for billions of years. And as it
grew it changed and changed, becoming harmony.

And like the ringing of a bell,*
        new galaxies were born,
With stars and moons and asteroids,
        new planets there as well.

        All made of sound, in harmony, but with no one there to hear.

        Well . . . not yet.

These planets spread throughout the world
        Like seeds spread in a field,
And where the harmony rang most true,
        New life began to yield.*

Bacteria came bubbling up for all that it was worth,
As life began from seeds of sound upon this blue-green earth.

Bacteria had quite an appetite.
        They ate rock and sky and sun,
And gave the earth so much in turn,
        Like air to breathe, yes, oxygen.

So when you see that mold on bread,
        that mold is not inferior,
It gave us air to breathe,
        please honor our bacteria.

All sorts of creatures crawled on the earth
        With sounds like eeek and grrrr,
And everything that could make sound,
        Made sounds so all could hear.

They grew ears to hear and eyes to see,
    They could hear the sounds, but not the harmony.

    Not yet, not yet.

The sound that with a bell began.*
    Now crawled and creeped and splashed and swam.
Snakes and spiders, bugs and bees,
    Birds that sang and cats that sneezed.

Then bears and monkeys joined the dance,
    And pandas too with baggy pants.
They held their young and watched them play
    Unlike the reptile in an earlier day.

The mammals laughed and loved and smiled,
    There was a bond between mother and child.
A mother primate sang out one night
    Because her child was in a fright.
Her voice went ah and oo and oh,
    Her song was simple, calm, and low.

The child then echoed what he heard,
    A song was born without a word.
This human child grew tall and strong
    And sang and danced all day long.

His ahs and oos and ees and ohs
    Turned into words like knees and toes.

Then other voices joined the song and chanted to the sky
    Their singing caused a harmony that made their spirits fly,
And for the first time on this earth, a human now could know

    That harmony was in all things, it made Creation flow.
    And this is why we're here,

    To know the harmony of things,
    Of stars and moons, of hens and mice,
    To hear earth's sound advice:

    That we are made of music too,
    And when we sing, we are the bell that made us true.*

So sing in praise of roaring rivers,
And dance until the planet quivers,
    And celebrate that we are here
    To look and touch and feel and hear
        The harmony of all the world as one,*
        And dream of what we can become.

Music and Learning

We NEED music. Throughout millions of years of evolving into humans, we have needed music. Music has been an essential part of our evolution. Music is especially important for the children in our schools. They are the reason I have written this book. Our children simply must have music in their lives—it is an imperative (Lloyd-Mayer and Langstaff 1995, 3–11; Brewer and Campbell 1991, 10–25).

Music charges the brain, energizing it like a million-volt battery (Brewer and Campbell 1991, 19–20). For several years, I taught a college class that met once a week at dusk, a time when the body wants to shut down. The students were studying to be teachers, and they spent their days doing student teaching at local schools. They were exhausted when they came to class. My challenge was to keep them awake and active for three hours despite their instinctive urge to rest. How did I do it? We sang. Every thirty minutes or so, we would sing a song. The singing, combined with the increased air to the lungs and brain, revived them. Singing electrifies the minds of people of all ages. Young school children return from recess fully charged. Yes, they have been exercising and playing, but they also have been yelling, chanting, and making a lot of noise. That sound charges the brain.

At special choir schools, children sing and do music for three or four hours every day. They engage in sports and play activities for two hours. This leaves only a few hours for their academic studies. Because the brains and bodies of these children are so highly charged from the singing and

37

exercising, they are able to learn in a short time what students in other kinds of schools take a full day to learn. And, sadly, I have seen the opposite effect in children who never sing or do any music at school or at home. The teachers of these students sometimes lament that the students aren't very bright and that they are not interested in their schoolwork.

Alfred Tomatis, a French throat and ear specialist, tells the story of a group of monks in a monastery who stopped singing in an effort to manage their busy schedules better. But the monks began to tire at their tasks—many became ill. Dr. Tomatis suggested that they start singing again. They did, and everyone was revitalized (Gilmore, Madaule, and Thompson 1989, 210–12).

By charging the brain, singing serves a basic function—it satisfies the hunger for mental stimulation. The hunger for creating sound and music is important to foster in education because it translates into a hunger for learning. The child who no longer hungers for sound no longer yearns to learn—the child is often bored. The child who sings is mentally stimulated. When I directed choruses in elementary and secondary schools, I would wonder why so many of the A students wanted to be in the choruses. I later realized that perhaps I had it backward. By singing in the choruses, the students were charging their brains, making A work more possible.

The ability to sing involves the ability to hear sounds inside the head. This is called *inner hearing* (Choksy 1981, 35–36). If you can hear a note, you can sing the note. It's that simple. Inner hearing is an essential mental process—everything from reading to problem solving requires inner hearing. Children learn to count out loud before they learn to count in their heads. Similarly, children learning to read must read out loud before they can internalize the sounds they see on the page. It is now believed that singing, especially for young children, is an aid to reading in that it strengthens the inner hearing process. Good inner hearing skills are also beneficial in problem solving tasks such as adding and multiplying (Brewer and Campbell 1991, 27–31, 35–36).

Music making is a powerful aid for the child learning to understand language, first as spoken sound and then as printed word recognition. Music making helps the child distinguish different sounds. With words, this means the ability to give meaning to the spoken word and later, the printed symbol of the word (Lloyd-Mayer and Langstaff 1995, 4).

Making music is a terrific aid in improving memory. Remember that most of us learned the alphabet by singing it first. And teachers today are bringing back the practice of teaching subjects through aural recitation—through song, poetry, and now rap. Children will learn lyrics much faster than they will learn cold facts. Teachers are using these techniques to teach everything from the multiplication table to historical events.

There is another reason why music is good for memory. Melodies and rhythms are basically patterns of sound. The ability to memorize these melodic and rhythmic patterns helps the brain remember other patterns—shapes, graphs, schedules, statistics, and the always important patterns of grammar and spelling. In addition, information learned through music, like singing "The Alphabet Song," becomes part of the permanant memory. We remember far longer than through non-musical learning (Lloyd-Meyer and Langstaff 1995, 10).

Our language is not made up of single words, but of words in sequences. There is a parallel between these word phrases and melodic phrases (Lloyd-Mayer and Langstaff 1995, 5-7). Just as we learn melodies with the stresses or accents on different notes, we speak and read with accents on different syllables and words. Imagine how dull and monotonous our speech would be without our inherent musicality to give it animation.

When we sing and make music, we are using both sides of the brain—both the logical and the creative side. The more we sing, the more we strengthen the communication between the two sides of the brain (Campbell 1989, 66–67). Too often this connection has atrophied, and learning has become one-sided.

In addition to coordinating the two sides of the brain, music making is important in coordinating the body. Balance is a function of the ear. Whatever strengthens the ear, strengthens balance. Elderly people often lose their sense of balance. Singing strengthens the ears and improves balance (Gilmore, Madaule, and Thompson 1989, 11, 38–39, 148–49). Children in almost every culture of the world do repetitive singing games involving jumping, skipping, and running. Their coordination is strengthened through these kinds of music making. Thus, skills like handwriting are aided by the rhythm/movement activities that accompany singing in young children (Lloyd-Mayer and Langstaff 1995, 7–8).

Sound production is good for the body. When we sing in a group, we can feel the vibrations on our skin and in our internal organs. We are receiving a marvelous massage of sound, both inside and out. As mentioned in chapter 2, sound stimulates the chakra points of the body. These chakra points can be found from the groin area to the top of the head. Information about chakras relates to auras (energy fields surrounding the body) and other not-proven phenomena, but there are some easily proven and understood points.

Remember the exercise where you chant various vowel tones in order to become sensitive to where your body "hears" the vibrations?

Some holistic healers believe that the body needs a full spectrum of sounds to be healthy (McClellan 1991, 38–44). We need low sounds, which affect the lower parts of the body; and we need high sounds, which affect the brain. A Buddhist monk trained in overtone singing can chant three notes at the same time—low, medium, and high. Women have high voices and men have low voices. Having high and low voices may be nature's way of providing a full spectrum of healing sounds when we sing together.

Making music requires making rhythms, whether we are singing or playing instruments. The ability to sustain a rhythm, to feel the pulse both physically and mentally, is extremely important for learning. Ultimately, the ability to sustain a rhythm helps a child sustain the rhythm of learning. Rhythms are a subtle but constant part of a child's learning environment. For example, there is the day-to-day rhythm of a schedule of activities. A child adjusts to such a schedule; there is a rhythm to these activities. And there are other rhythms of learning. The ability to concentrate on an activity such as quiet reading requires a child to sustain an inner rhythm without giving up. Children who can sustain spoken, sung, marched, or played rhythms can also sustain mental activities such as reading (Brewer and Campbell 1991, 150–53).

Any repeated cycle creates a rhythm. The heartbeat is an example of this. The human body has many rhythms going on simultaneously—digestive rhythms, sleep rhythms, breath rhythms, and various brain wave rhythms. The rhythms of the body can be influenced through music. You can change the heartbeat, the breathing patterns, even the brain waves of the mind. Is it wrong to manipulate the body and mind through music to increase learning? As long as one uses the powers of music for positive purposes, these powers should be taken advantage of.

We learn through seeing, hearing, feeling—through all the senses. Musical intelligence, with its many benefits, must be part of the total learning environment. But there is more.

Children learn social skills through singing. When a five-year-old sings a game song where there are strict rules, the child is dealing with issues of cooperation and fairness. Let's say a party game song requires that a leader goes to the center of the circle to do a series of activities. The child in the outer circle learns to accept the rules of the game, particularly the hard fact that his or her turn may not come.

Music making can build communities, whether these communities are schools or entire cultures. If you've ever sung along with a national anthem when the flag is raised at an Olympic award ceremony, then you know how powerful community singing can be. Jailed civil rights activists in South Africa are told to be quiet, but they sing instead. The singing brings them together; it unites and intensifies their community. By singing together they become extremely powerful, a communal bond is forged, uniting them and creating a common power far more powerful than that of the guards who hold the keys to their freedom.

Singing brings people together and helps form group identities. By identifying with groups, individuals draw on the strength of the community, becoming stronger through singing. Children who sing in the classroom or in school assemblies draw a sense of power from the experience. The singing helps to intensify their identity as members of that classroom or school. They come to see themselves as learners within a powerful learning environment.

In Conclusion

Music is an amazing power in our lives. Music has been necessary for our evolution, and if we wish to continue to evolve we must continue to make music—not secondhand music, but firsthand music. It is not good enough to stand by and listen to others. We must each make music ourselves. Children especially must have music making in their lives—singing, dancing, and playing instruments.

Both the multicultural and the multiple intelligence movements are part of a broader holistic movement that asks a pertinent question, "How great is our human potential?" Is this it? Or are we capable of more?

I now believe that if we embrace the powers of music from the diverse cultural traditions of the world, and if we embrace the powers of music as revealed by the new story of creation, the realization of our human potential will become truly unlimited.

SING and SHINE ON!

This song is our song,
It's your song, it's my song

As long as we live
We'll shine and we'll sing on

Live to shine,
Love living the song.
Live to love,
Sing and Shine On!

How Do We
Teach
Songs?

5

Four Simple Rules

CONFIDENCE IS one piece of the foundation to singing well. Here are some easy-to-incorporate guidelines that will help establish this swaying confidence:

- Rule One: Make every group sound fantastic.
- Rule Two: Make everyone feel confident through creating a supportive environment.
- Rule Three: Teach songs as if you were teaching them to yourself.
- Rule Four: Honor cultural traditions.

Rule One: Make Every Group Sound Fantastic

A class of fifth graders follows as their teacher leads a rousing folk song. The students are singing in several different keys. Most of them don't know the words very well, and they have no idea what the song is about. The class sounds pretty bad, but the teacher, full of enthusiasm, continues to sing away. Why do the students sound bad? Because the teacher is allowing them to sound bad. What will happen if the teacher continues to allow mediocrity? The students won't want to sing anymore.

Not one of us, no matter what our age, enjoys doing anything poorly. Where's the fun in that? A boy tries to shoot a basket. Time and again he fails. The basket is too high, and the ball too heavy. He quits in frustration.

Do you blame him? I don't. I was one of those people who couldn't shoot baskets to save my life, and I was the tallest one in my class. I was taller than the teachers! If someone had taken the time to show me how to shoot a basket, I would have enjoyed it. I was allowed to fail. If someone had given the boy mentioned above a lighter ball and a lower basket, he would have started getting baskets. He may even have come to love basketball and to look forward to playing it.

I guarantee you that if you can get your students to sing well—in tune, with energy, and with an understanding of the significance of the music— you will receive nothing but enthusiasm from them.

Older boys are often the first to lose interest in singing. I am convinced that when you teach that older boy to sound great, singing music that he can identify with, he will love singing. When I taught general music in grades K-8, I put special emphasis on making the boys sound great. I even had them perform publicly as a group.

The changing voice is a major concern for older boys, one that should not be ignored. There will be fewer and fewer notes that sound good. It is essential, therefore, that those few notes sound great and that the songs they sing use only these notes.

If your class has serious intonation problems (singing out of tune) you will need to work on this all the time. Review chapter 9.

Following Rule One doesn't mean that every group has to sound like the Vienna Choir Boys. Nor does it mean that you can't do the occasional silly song that you know will sound terrible, but will be lots of fun to sing. The rule simply reminds us that we are more amazing than we realize.

Why expect anything less than wonderful, bright, shining voices from children? It is too easy to say, "They are only children," or, "Children are supposed to sound squeaky and out of tune." The attitude behind this kind of thinking suggests that children are merely mediocre versions of adults. I am eternally grateful to every teacher I ever had who made me excel, who made me reach my full potential. We owe the same to our students.

Rule Two: Make Everyone Feel Confident Through Creating a Supportive Environment

Learning a new song can be a major source of frustration, or it can be a powerful source of pride—for both teacher and student alike. Consider, for example, these two scenarios; and consider them, for now, from the student's point of view.

You are faced by a well-meaning teacher who is about to teach you a song that you have never heard before. The song "De Colores" is in Spanish. The teacher begins by singing a long phrase and then asks you and your classmates to repeat it. You all try but just can't remember the words. Instead of repeating the difficult first phrase, the teacher goes on to the second phrase. You begin to look around the room to see if anyone else is able to do it. You find that you are not alone. Everyone is stumbling. Yet, the teacher now asks the class to sing the entire song! You and your classmates experience a mix of emotions. You feel frustrated because you can't seem to learn the song. You begin to feel resentment and anger toward the teacher for not being able to teach you. You certainly have lost all interest in learning the song, and you may have begun to lose interest in music in general. Your teacher can now work with all the energy of Zeus but will have trouble getting more than a mumbled whisper out of anyone. Now, as you think about this scenario, keep in mind that the teacher is truly well meaning, sincerely wanting you and your classmates to be able to learn and enjoy the song.

Let's start again with a different scenario. You are faced with an equally well-meaning teacher; yet this teacher begins by smiling and talking energetically about a singing tradition among Mexican Americans in Southern California. You find yourself drawn in by what the teacher is saying. Then the teacher sings "De Colores." Before you have time to decide that the song is impossible to learn, you find yourself speaking some of the words. You repeat after the teacher. A few mistakes are made. The teacher corrects you, then goes over the words again. By now, you're feeling pretty good, and the teacher amplifies this by complimenting your pronunciation. You and your classmates sit up, receptive to the teacher's next move. Soon you are singing short phrases, then longer phrases. Everyone is now engaged and feeling good about the experience of learning the song. Eventually, the class stands and sings the entire song in Spanish. There is a burst of joy and delight as everyone breaks out in applause. Smiles abound.

Now, what was the difference between these two scenarios? For me, the difference can be summed up in one word: confidence. The students in the successful second scenario felt confident about their abilities from the start. The teacher, by building their confidence, made them want to move ahead at each and every stage. Had they, like the students in the first scenario, felt frustrated in learning the words or the melodies, they would have taken the all too familiar path of becoming confused or bored, followed by a feeling of general antagonism toward singing.

These two scenarios help to illustrate why all students, from the shy wallflower to the class jester, must attain a feeling of confidence in themselves. An entire song cannot be put together until everyone in the class feels confident about every single phrase. But, you may argue, isn't repeating phrases over and over again boring? Won't the students lose interest? No, that hasn't been my experience. As long as singers feel confident in themselves, they will not be bored. To be on the safe side, however, there are some tricks you can use to hold students' interest while they are learning some of the more difficult songs (see instructions for teaching "Building Bridges" in chapter 7).

Feeling safe is essential for each child—safe to make mistakes, safe to excel. We all have witnessed the student who didn't dare do well at something for fear that the rest of the students would make fun of her. We have also seen the student who has climbed back into his shell after having made a mistake in front of his fellow students. For the sake of these kinds of students, it is essential that the teacher create a supportive environment.

A supportive environment is one in which everyone is expected to sing to the best of his or her ability; making mistakes is welcome as long as expectations for fixing them are high. Smiling and having fun should always be part of learning songs, but laughter in the form of ridicule has no place in a supportive environment. Forms of negativity tear down confidence more quickly than anything else. In a supportive environment, there can't be enough positive reinforcement from the teacher. Let your students know after each phrase that they did it very well. I sometimes use visual signals such as the "okay" hand signal or the gesture of polishing my fingernails on my lapel. Even the smallest gesture can fill young singers with positive feelings about themselves.

Children sing best when they are standing close to each other. I prefer a circle or a semicircle of chairs, with lots of standing and moving to keep the body fully involved. There will always be some students who are stronger singers than others. These strong singers should be encouraged to sing out. Be careful, however, not to have all the strong singers clumped together. Remember that everyone is potentially a strong singer. If you spread out your strong singers, your less confident singers will get some support. Support among students is a beautiful thing. Encourage students to help and praise each other. This doesn't mean you should ask students to pat each other on the back all the time. Simple forms of compliments like applause will do.

By creating a supportive environment and by fostering confidence in each child, you will be setting the stage for something miraculous to happen. Have you ever experienced children singing–when they seemed to sparkle with energy, when their eyes shone with radiance, and when their voices brought tears to your eyes? Children at this point have gone beyond confidence to something I call "wonder and awe." It is a transcendent state in which they are literally in awe of the sounds and energies they are creating. Those listening are often in awe as well. This stage of *wonder-full* singing can only be reached through building confidence in each child.

Rule Three: Teach Songs as if You Were Teaching Them to Yourself

Along with being supportive, it is also essential that you be sensitive to the limitations of your students. I always teach a song as if I were teaching it to myself. This kind of attitude communicates three messages to the singers. The first is that they need not fear that I will confuse them or bring their confidence down in any way. The second is that I will understand any difficulties they have in learning the song and will sympathize with their struggles. The third is that I consider their learning abilities to be not all that different from mine; in other words, all of us have similar abilities to learn the song and to learn it amazingly well.

You never want to intimidate your students. Though seldom intentional, intimidation is a frequent reason for students' shying away from singing. Imagine this nightmare scenario: A teacher sings in a huge operatic voice, full of vibrato, tacitura, and all that fancy stuff. The teacher then asks the students to sing along. I guarantee that the students will feel intimidated by the teacher's voice. Sing with a natural confident voice. Students will echo your confidence.

I have been teaching teachers to lead songs for many years. The most common mistake that song leaders make is teaching a song too quickly. To avoid this, constantly ask yourself question like this, "If I were in my students' place, would I need to have that last line repeated?" The answer will not always be yes, but most of the time the repetition will help. Also, consider this kind of situation: You have taught the first phrase of a song, then the second, then the third, and finally the fourth. If I were learning the song, I would have completely forgotten the first line at this point. So, when you have finished with the fourth phrase, go back and teach the first phrase again.

Do a little *calling out*. After you have gone through each phrase a few times, do an entire verse; but at the end of each phrase, call out the first words of the next phrase as a gentle reminder. For example, if you were teaching Woodie Guthrie's "This Land Is Your Land," the class would sing, "This land is your land, this land is my land." At this point the teacher would call out the words, "From California . . ." This simple reminder of the next line is a big help. It is another example of teaching a song as if you were teaching it to yourself.

If you are teaching a harmony part to older students, you will need to constantly reinforce each part with positive repetition. I often see song leaders teaching the melody and the harmony and then putting the two parts together, only to find that the melody group has forgotten their part. Here's a simple trick. Once you have taught the melody and the harmony, put them together slowly. Have the melody group sing the verse a few times by themselves. It is important that they be able to sing it without you, otherwise they will get into the bad habit of only singing what you sing. On their second time through, sing the harmony part yourself so the melody group doesn't get thrown off by the harmony. When the melody group is finally comfortable with their part, ask the harmony group to join in. They have already heard you singing their part a few times with the melody group, so it will be easy for them to join in. When doing this procedure, don't stop between repetitions. Keep up the repetition, adding the harmony as you go.

Warning: Too much repetition can condition students to need it more and more. Sometimes I will say, "I'm going to give you each line twice, and that's it. You've got to learn it." A little positive pressure never hurt anyone. I don't apply this kind of pressure often, though, because learning songs can sometimes be enough pressure and because not all students learn in the same way—some may need visual or kinetic reinforcement.

Also, remember that not all songs have to be taught in one sitting. You may break a song up and teach a different part each day. Be sure to follow

Rule One with each song fragment, however—it must sound fantastic. If it doesn't the students may not want to learn the next part the next day.

When I apply the first three rules in my song leading, I always get great results. A confident and supportive environment fosters powerful singing, especially when the song leader takes into account the strengths and limitations of the singers.

Rule Four: Honor Cultural Traditions

Until a few years ago, the idea that music was somehow tied to cultural identity was as foreign to me as the notion that embracing cultural traditions brings power to music. I had been working with music of many cultures for a long time and had gained firsthand knowledge of both black gospel and Jewish musical traditions through my work with the Chicago Children's Choir and other sources. But it wasn't until I took workshops with Ysaye Maria Barnwell that the importance of musical tradition took hold. Ysaye Maria Barnwell sings with the African American women's vocal group Sweet Honey in the Rock. This group is based in Washington, DC, and travels the world performing music from the African and African American traditions. Ysaye never teaches a song without first having given a thorough explanation of the tradition behind the song, often with the help of historian George Brandon. For example, when she taught the song "Woke Up This Mornin'" (see chapter 7) she and George first discussed the many civil rights songs that had been based on old spirituals. They then described the environment in which the song might have been sung. By the time we sang the song, we felt as if we were in a Southern church surrounded by a row of National Guardsmen and an angry mob intent on burning us out. We sang the song with a newfound intensity—an intensity born of the tradition itself.

I felt a similar intensity when I studied with Joseph Shabalala. Joseph is the leader of the South African group Ladysmith Black Mambazo, who performed with Paul Simon on his *Graceland* album. Joseph spent a long time discussing the rich traditions behind the songs he taught. Without an understanding of these traditions, the songs would have become empty, without meaning (see Joseph Shabalala's song "Thula Klizeo" in chapter 6).

My studies with Ysaye, George, and Joseph led me to study ethnomusicology, which is simply the study of music in its connection with culture. The prominent themes in current ethnomusicological studies relate to cultural identity and to music's role in creating that identity.

As a lighthearted example of the connection between music and culture, let's look back to our high school years. What kind of music did we listen to? What did we wear? How did we talk? Looking back, I am able to see the connections between the music that individuals listened to and the groups they hung out with. To oversimplify, there were "Dead-Heads" who could be identified by their long hair and headbands. There were greasers with leather jackets who listened to fifties rock. There were teeny-boppers who listened to bubble gum rock. There were folkies, jazz beatniks, and even the occasional few who listened to what their parents listened to. In each case, the music helped to define who they were. Music helps give us our identity.

At my twentieth high school reunion, I found that most of my friends were still listening to the same kind of music they had listened to twenty years before. Their identities were secure, there was no need for change. Some, however, had branched out and were exploring the incredible diversity of today's music. These friends' identities had changed with the new music they listened to. They were adapting to a changing world.

Think also of how, since the 1950s, rock and roll has represented the music of rebellion to the youth of the world. The rebelliousness of the music has given identity to a rebellious culture. And a new phenomenon has developed. For the young people of almost every culture on earth, rock and roll has become the music of choice—the music to identify with. Two Czechoslovakian students once told me of how, under Communist rule, their musical tastes had been dictated by the government. Traditional folk music had been banned. All "folk music" was actually composed by government sponsored university composers as a way to foster national pride. When Communist rule ended, the youth were suddenly free to create their own musical identities, but instead of reaching back for their traditional Czechoslovakian roots, they reached out for the rock and roll of the rest of the world.

A South African friend told me a similar story. As restrictions were lifted in her nation, young people had more and more choices. But instead of choosing music of their Zulu and Xhosa traditions, they chose rock and roll. It is a global phenomenon. The youth of Boston and Los Angeles do not identify with sacred harp music or spirituals. Instead they identify with rock, rap, and hip-hop. The indigenous folk music of most cultures is slowly disappearing, preserved for posterity by avid ethnomusicologists. Pop music has become global—it is the new universal folk music—world music. This music is rock, reggae, juju, hip-hop, and rap. World music is simply the modern manifestation of a very old tradition—that of the music of one culture merging with the music of another. Paul Simon's *Graceland* album blends South African, zydeco, and rock styles. Sunny King Ade of Nigeria blends Hawaiian, Nigerian, Jamaican, and rock elements. The results are very exciting. They point the way to a new internationalism, a new global awareness with a new global music that helps to create a new global identity—one in which our diversity makes us stronger, not weaker.

Contemporary composers such as Philip Glass and Steve Reich use elements of Hindu ragas and Indonesian gamelan music in their compositions, just as Mozart used Turkish elements in his music two hundred years ago.

There is a danger, however, that comes with this new global identity. Many in the mass culture feel that their music is to be shared with everyone, therefore all music is to be shared with everyone. But there are cultures that do not want their music shared, particularly their sacred music. The music of the Navaho Nightway Ritual, for example, belongs to a very definite place and time. Removed from that place and time, let's say brought to a school classroom, the music becomes inappropriate. Such music is integral to its ritual and may not be used out of context.

Many Native Americans, having lost their land and much of their tradition, feel that it is the final theft to have their sacred music and their spirituality itself stolen, even by well-intentioned people. There is, however, Navaho music that may be taught. We should, therefore, not be afraid to celebrate the music of diverse cultures, but we must be aware of and honor and preserve the sacred traditions of all cultures.

This honoring of traditions, as I have said, makes singing very powerful. In honoring the traditions, we become connected to the cultures they come from. And we become connected to them in terms of time and place, often to long-ago times and distant places. To feel this kind of connectedness is extremely powerful.

When I taught music at the K-8 school in Cambridge, I taught everyone the anthem of the African National Congress, "N'Kosi Sikeleli Afrika" ("Bless, Oh Lord, Our Country Africa")—now one of two official anthems of South Africa. For me, this is perhaps the most powerful song on earth. The composer of this great anthem was Enoch Sontonga, a Zulu who had trained in England to become a teacher. Returning to his home in South Africa, Sontonga was told by the authorities that he would be allowed to sing only songs and hymns from the European tradition with his students. Forced to comply with this ruling, Sontonga was still able to write a piece of music that was instilled with African pride; it is the music that is now the beginning of "N'Kosi Sikeleli

Afrika." Sontonga was able to get away with this because, although the words spoke distinctly to the hearts of the African people, the melody itself sounded very European—some claim the melody is an old Methodist hymn.

N'kosi Sikeleli Afrika
Bless Oh Lord Our Country Africa
by Enoch Sontonga
words adapted by Judith Cook Tucker

Moderate with Energy

Bless, oh Lord our coun- try   A - fri- ca.   So that all may see her
N'ko- si   si- ke- lel-   i   A- fri- ka   Ma- lu- pha- ka- nyi- sw'u-

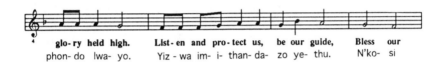

glo- ry held high.   List- en and pro- tect us,   be our guide,   Bless   our
phon- do lwa- yo.   Yiz - wa im- i- than- da- zo ye- thu.   N'ko- si

Mo - ther   A - fri - ca,   Ti - na   lu - sa- po   lwa-   yo.
si- ke- le-   la

Sontonga's song eventually grew in popularity and was sung by children throughout southern Africa. Later, the South African Xhosa poet SEK Mqhayi added another verse. Then, when the African National Congress was formed, "N'Kosi Sikeleli Afrika" became its anthem. Under apartheid, however, the song was banned. In defiance, proud South Africans have often stood and sung their anthem at funerals and at other public occasions.

Whenever I teach "N'Kosi Sikeleli Afrika," I make the singers aware of the anthem's tradition and power. And, as with all anthems, those who sing it must stand, giving the song the complete respect it commands.

A former student thanked me a while ago for teaching him "N'Kosi Sikeleli Afrika." He said that he had just heard a choir singing the great anthem as part of a visit to Boston by the South African leader Nelson Mandela. My student said that because he knew the song and its tradition, he felt personally connected with the people of South Africa. This sense of connectedness is powerful and beautiful, and it cannot be taught; it can only be experienced on an emotional level. By feeling emotionally connected with other people in the world, we expand our own worlds. Whenever you teach your students about a musical tradition, make sure you represent the tradition as a vital, living force, not as something dead from the past. Meaningless traditions don't survive Only the traditions that make us better people survive.

Naturally, the anthems of our own countries, great songs like "O Canada," "Lift Every Voice and Sing," and "The Star Spangled Banner" should be taught. These songs have long and fascinating histories. The traditions behind the anthems help to make them powerful.

There need not be a division between those who believe in the use of multicultural music and those who believe in supporting the traditional music we have taught in schools for many years. We need to accept that all music, including the music of the traditionalists, belongs to a culture. All music fits under the umbrella of multicultural music. We need to celebrate the music of all cultures, including the music of whatever our own culture is.

The traditionalists can no longer claim the music of Johann Sebastian Bach and other classical European composers as being the norm or the standard upon which to base music education. Most students today know as little about Bach as they know about the spirituals. Both need to be taught—taught with an emphasis on embracing the cultures behind the music. I teach almost all songs from a cultural perspective, even the music of Bach. Young people don't hate Bach, they hate people who like Bach. They dislike the culture of Bach. By explaining Bach's culture and making it exciting and meaningful, I have a strong chance in helping students identify with the music of Bach.

There is another reason why those in favor of multiculturalism and the traditionalists need to unite. Both movements wish to preserve traditions . . . traditions that are threatened by the global pop phenomenon. Yes, this new World Music is exciting and valid, but its allure is powerful. We need a world where the new mass music and the old, highly diverse cultural traditions can exist side by side.

Final Considerations

This chapter and the previous chapters have introduced a philosophy for song teaching and a vision of the potential of powerful singing. With this vision, it is easier to set goals and to achieve the desired amazing results.

As I see it, the goal of song teaching is to create a supernova of human energy. I use this analogy because a supernova is a star that can no longer hold its energy within itself; it has to let it go, it has to explode with all the energy that has been held within. Powerful singing gives people the chance to release the energy that can no longer be held within. This energy is emotional energy, physical energy, communal energy, and a kind of energy that connects us to the entire creative universe.

This supernova of energy can be achieved through *a cappella* singing—singing without the support of instruments such as pianos or guitars—singing with one's fullest energy. It is singing in harmony, both the harmony of music and the metaphorical harmony of living systems. It is singing that is supported by thousands of years of cultural traditions and millions of years of evolution. It is singing with joy, awe, compassion, and creativity.

I have found that powerful singing can best be done in a certain kind of environment. The ideal physical space is a room with movable chairs, plenty of natural light, and good ventilation. I prefer to have the chairs placed in a semicircle or circle. Everyone has eye contact with everyone else, and the singers can hear one another quite well.

I often end my singing celebrations by removing the chairs and having everyone stand in a circle, sometimes many rows deep. This is when the energy really erupts.

6

Basic Strategy for Rote Song Teaching

· LEARNING SONGS by ear is the basic strategy for teaching most, but not all songs. Learning songs through music reading is also an essential skill, but one better suited to the music specialist. There are six simple steps for teaching songs by rote:

1. Introduce the song.
2. Perform the song with energy.
3. Phrase by phrase, have singers echo you, the leader. If the song is in an unfamiliar language, start with speaking the words only, then singing them.
4. Have singers sing the entire verse or verse section.
5. Correct mistakes when they happen.
6. At some point, talk about the tradition from which the song comes and/or talk about the meaning of the song.

The order of these steps can vary. Because every song is different, the strategy for teaching each song will be a little different.

As an example, here is how I teach "Thula Klizeo."

1. I introduce the song with information such as the following. "Thula Klizeo" is a song by Joseph Shabalala of the group Ladysmith Black Mambazo. This is a South African group that became world famous when they toured and recorded with Paul Simon in the late 1980s. Joseph Shabalala, the group's leader, wrote "Thula Klizeo" on a visit to New York. At that moment, he

Thula Klizeo By Joseph Shabalala

Thu- la Kli - zi - o,   Na- la- pa-sey Ki - ya.   Ey   Ki - ya,

Na - la - pa - sey   Ki - ya

was homesick for South Africa and he missed his fourteen children, whom, because of the unfair apartheid laws at that time, he did not know if he would ever see again. Joseph Shabalala, however, was calmed by the thought, "Be still my heart, even here I am at home," and these words became the song; but the song means much more, as you will see in a moment.

2. I perform the song with energy, giving everyone an idea of how it sounds. I know that at this point some students will be thinking, "This is too hard for me to learn," so before the potential supernovas can sink into despair, I go on to the next step. I sometimes avoid any potential intimidation by doing step two after step three. It is important to perform the song at some point, otherwise the students will only have heard song fragments. They won't know how the whole song should sound.

3. I speak the words of the song, word by word.

Leader: Thula! [too' lah]
Group: Thula!

I repeat this, and as I want more energy from the class, I shout the words with an enthusiastic smile.

Leader: Thula!
Group: Thula!

Everyone should be smiling at this point. Now I go on and speak another word.

Leader: klizeo [kleh zee' oh]
Group: klizeo
Leader: Thula klizeo
Group: Thula klizeo

Leader: na la pa [nah lah pah']
Group: na la pa

Leader: na la pa
Group: na la pa

Leader: sey ki-ya! [say kah'-ee yah]
Group: sey ki-ya!
Leader: sey ki-ya!
Group: sey ki-ya!

This may seem like a lot of repetition, but don't forget that you must teach the song as if you were teaching it to yourself. If you were in the students' seats, would you be able to remember all these words in an unfamiliar language with just one repetition? I continue the repetitions, now with complete phrases. I use the same rhythms that they will be singing in a few moments. So, for example, when I say "na la pa sey ki-ya," the "ki" is held twice as long as the other syllables.

Leader: Thula klizeo
Group: Thula klizeo
Leader: Thula klizeo
Group: Thula klizeo

Leader: na' la pa' sey ki'-ya
Group: na la pa sey ki-ya

It is important to listen as the students repeat after you. It is easy to hear mistakes. I hear that some students are having trouble with "na la pa." They are saying "na la la" instead. So I break it up again, and accent the p.

Leader: na la *pa*
Group: na la pa

Leader: na la *pa* sey ki-ya
Group: na la pa sey ki-ya

Leader: hey ki-ya [hay kah-ee yah]
Group: hey ki-ya

Leader: na' la pa' sey ki'-ya
Group: na la pa sey ki-ya

At this point I choose to go over all the words again. I don't want to teach the melody until each singer feels confident with all the words. I cannot stress this enough—that the singers must feel one hundred percent confident at this stage of learning the song. You will be wasting time if you go on without their confidence. You may end up after a long period of time having to start again, but by then the energy may have gone and the singers' trust in you may have diminished considerably.

4. Once each singer is feeling sufficiently confident with the words, I go on to teach the melody. I sing the whole song, slowly at first, so that everyone can become familiar with the notes; and I make sure that I sing it in a range that is comfortable for everyone—not too high and not too low. This is very important. If the midrange of a song is between middle C and G (five notes higher) you are in a safe range for all. (See chapter 11.)

I go on, this time singing a few words at a time, asking students to repeat after me until they are comfortable.

> Leader: (singing slowly) Thula klizeo
> Group: Thula klizeo
> Leader: Thula klizeo
> Group: Thula klizeo

> Leader: na la pa sey ki-ya
> Group: na la pa sey ki-ya

5. I notice that some are having trouble singing "sey ki-ya", so I isolate these notes and have everyone repeat them. Making mistakes when learning a song is very natural. No one should ever be made to feel inadequate or stupid for making a mistake. If the mistake is not fixed at this point, however, it may never be fixed. With younger children it may be impossible to correct a mistake once it has been learned. It is important, therefore, to get into the habit of correcting mistakes immediately, with kindness and clarity. I even go so far as to act as if I didn't notice the mistake. I don't want to do anything to diminish their confidence. I simply have them repeat the phrase with more care.

I find that ultimately, by teaching a song slowly and carefully, the students learn it faster. If I were to teach this song quickly, many mistakes would occur. There would be confusion. I would end up spending more time trying to reteach it later. Uninspired singing would be the result.

Now I continue to combine the words and melody, giving a "stop" signal with my hands to indicate that students should wait until I've finished each grouping before repeating after me.

> Leader: (singing) sey ki-ya
> Group: sey ki-ya

> Leader: na la pa sey ki-ya
> Group: na la pa sey ki-ya

> Leader: hey ki-ya

Group: hey ki-ya

Leader: na la pa sey ki-ya
Group: na la pa sey ki-ya

Leader: hey ki-ya
Group: hey ki-ya

Leader: na la pa sey ki-ya
Group: hey ki-ya

Next, I sing complete phrases and ask students to repeat after me.

Leader: Thula klizeo, na la pa sey ki-ya
Group: Thula klizeo, na la pa sey ki-ya

Leader: Thula klizeo, na la pa sey ki-ya
Group: Thula klizeo, na la pa sey ki-ya

Leader: hey ki-ya, na la pa sey ki-ya
Group: hey ki-ya, na la pa sey ki-ya

Leader: hey ki-ya, na la pa sey ki-ya
Group: hey ki-ya, na la pa sey ki-ya

Once all the singers sound confident, I indicate that it is time to try the whole song. We speed up the tempo to the correct speed.

All: Thula klizeo, na la pa sey ki-ya

Leader: (I say "repeat" or "again" at the end of the phrase.)

All: Thula klizeo, na la pa sey ki-ya

Leader: hey ki-ya (This reminds them of the next phrase. I
    speak all of these reminders in tempo. In other words, the song
    never slows down or stops.)

All: hey ki-ya, na la pa sey ki-ya

Leader: Repeat

All: hey ki-ya, na la pa sey ki-ya

We then repeat the whole song again. If the energy is right, there is often a spontaneous burst of applause at this point. There may be some in the group, particularly in a group of older students, who can sing harmonies. Singing in harmony should always be encouraged. As the leader, you should sing a combination of melody and harmony. I do this in a very simple way. On the last held note of the phrase, I sing the melody note, then quickly jump to a harmony note. By singing the melody note, you help those who need to hear the melody. By adding the harmony note immediately afterward, you give others an idea of how to harmonize.

Thula Klizeo by Joseph Shabalala

Thu- la Kli- zi - o,   Na- la- pa- sey Ki - ya.

Leader: Add harmony.

Now everyone sings the melody again, and some begin to harmonize. Most don't. That's okay. There is a traditional dance that goes along with "Thula Klizeo." I introduce that dance at this point.

Leader: Ah, but there's more. It's time to learn the dance. In most parts of the world, people don't sit still while they sing. They move. They dance. Our dance goes like this:

It is a simple standing-in-place dance. The body is bent forward slightly. The feet do a walking-in-place motion to the beat with the right foot "stomping quietly" out in front. For the first two lines of text the hands echo the beat of the feet, simultaneously pulsing downwards at stomach level, palms facing down. Smile.

For the second phrase, "hey ki-ya," raise both hands in the air and then bring them back to the same motion as before. Every time you come to the phrase "hey ki-ya," lift the hands to heaven.

I ask everyone to stand, and immediately we do the dance and song together, with harmony if possible. Again, there is great excitement once the song has been sung through a few times. Now is a good time to give more information about the tradition behind the song.

6. Leader: For thousands of years the Zulu people of Southern Africa did great dances in which they kicked high in the air and stomped proudly on the earth. These were dances of great strength, defiance, and power. Under the system of apartheid, however, the Zulu people were not allowed to do their traditional dances. Nor were they allowed to show their power or defiance. If they showed power or defiance, they could easily

be locked up in jail. So they developed something called "Es-*káh*-tah-mee-yah," which means "to stomp quietly." That is what we do every time we put our right foot down. We show our anger and power. We are saying "No" to the apartheid system. We are showing our defiance in a way that will not get us locked up in jail. Since 1975, it has been the young people of South Africa who have publicly shown the most anger toward the apartheid system.

Let us now dance and sing the song again, and remember that even though the words mean, "Be still my heart, even here I am at home," the dance means, "We are powerful and no one can take that power from us." (I sometimes have the group repeat that last phrase after me.)

Providing this kind of information about the song's tradition adds an essential element that lends immense power to the singing. This is the power inherent in all cultural traditions. Tradition connects us with the past. In a way, tradition awakens our memories. By honoring traditions, we somehow remember experiences celebrated by our own ancestors. Our heritage comes alive in us. Many cultures, especially in Africa, believe that making music connects them with their ancestors.

When you discuss traditions with your students, remember to adapt the language and concepts to the age group you are addressing. The previous description, for example, is geared to children ten years old and older.

Do the song and dance again, this time repeating it for a long time. The song has a trancelike quality to it; and, like all chants, its power builds with repetition. A kind of trance state can actually result from this type of singing. Continue to let the energy build. Add percussive instruments if you want. Vary the dance movements by bending lower, stomping higher, or by making it into a march. Once learned, this song becomes infectious and will be very popular. It is a great energy booster, and it has universal appeal. Whenever a song like this is sung, however, don't let it become trivialized; its meaning and the power of its tradition must always be apparent. How would you feel if someone trivialized your cultural traditions?

Whatever song teaching technique is used, it is important to teach with energy. I teach classes and workshops in song leading, and one of the biggest problems I repeatedly observe is a teacher teaching with insufficient energy. A song teacher can follow every rule and have the most brilliant strategy for teaching a new song, but if his or her energy is low and he or she is singing in a lackluster fashion, the students will not learn the song well. They will merely mirror the low-energy teacher. A high-energy teacher, on the other hand, will generate high-energy results. In fact, I have seen high-energy teachers break every rule in the book, using little or no strategy, and still have wonderful results. One young song leader, a student of mine, sang three lines in Japanese with terrific energy, then asked everyone to repeat them. Normally the results would have been catastrophic. No one would have remembered the first word, let alone the entire three lines, but because of this young teacher's remarkable ability to sing with energy and to instill confidence and vitality in her students, the results were excellent. We sang the words just as she had sung them.

Just what does teaching with energy mean? It means singing clearly and exactly; not slurring the melody or stumbling over the rhythm. It means singing with good posture, feet on the floor. It means having good eye contact with the students. It means singing with resonance as opposed to singing with a dull, breathy tone. It means singing with a strong sense of forward motion, not letting the word phrases fade away, but letting them build. It means singing with percussive consonants as opposed to mushy pronunciations. Most importantly, energetic teaching means teaching with a sense of meaning, understanding the message of the song as well as its tradition. When the teacher is thrilled by a song, the students will be equally thrilled and will learn the song thrillingly.

7

More Song Teaching Strategies

EVERY SONG is different. Every group of people will be different. You will need to know a variety of song teaching strategies. You may use hand signs to teach a song one day, then the next day use the call and response technique for the same song. You may want to combine the call and response technique with the story technique. You have to use your intuition and creativity. Above all, remember the four rules discussed in chapter 5, starting with making everyone sound fantastic. Ultimately, it is that rule which will help you choose the best song teaching strategy.

Call and Response

The call and response song is a song in which the leader calls out a phrase and the group sings a response. This form of song can be found in a variety of styles all around the world. It is the easiest song teaching technique, and it is always exciting. This assumes that you, the teacher, are excited about the song and convey that excitement. As I said in the previous chapter, students will not only echo what you sing, but will also echo your energy.

The most common form of call and response song is one in which a leader sings something and the group echoes it exactly. A good example of this kind of song is Ella Jenkin's version of "Cadima," a cheerful patriotic song from Israel. The word *cadima* means to go forward and backward at the same time—to go forward with a strong respect for the traditions of the past. As I tell children, it's like a tree growing taller and wider, but also being deeply rooted in the earth.

Kadima
Arranged and Adapted as "Cadima" by Ella Jenkins
A Traditional Israeli Song

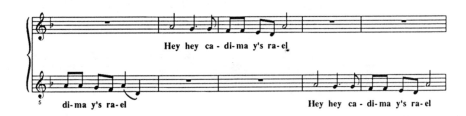

- 2 -

To lead this call and response song, you simply find the right range (not too high and not too low, b up to B), smile, and ask the students for an echo. Then sing each phrase, with the group echoing. At first, you may want to join them in the echo, but eventually you should have them do the echo on their own. If mistakes are made the first time through, it is okay to simply repeat the phrase or a part of the phrase until the singers sing it correctly.

Do this without getting off of the beat. In other words, don't stop the song to fix the mistakes, simply make the corrections part of the song. Because it is a folk song, you don't have to sing it the same way every time. Some phrases can be repeated more often if you wish, and the corrections you make can thus become part of the song.

Maintain a steady beat. If there is an interruption, a visitor to the room or a child asking a question, keep the pulse going. This principle is true for all call and response songs. You may want to tap the pulse on your knee.

Once a song like "Cadima" has been learned, it is fun to ask a student to lead it with everyone else following them. Call and response songs like "Cadima" are also great for singing celebrations. It's a great audience involvement song.

Sometimes you may want to turn a regular song into call and response. The song "Thula Klizeo" works well as a call and response song, especially with younger children who may have difficulty learning the whole song in Zulu. You begin, "Thula klizeo." They echo, "Thula klizeo." You continue, "Na-la-pa-sey-ki-ya." They echo, "Na-la-pa-sey-ki-ya." Keep a steady beat as you continue with this great song. Repeat it as long as you wish. Add the dance. Make up motions.

It is easy to make up call and response songs. Using two or three simple notes (such as sol, mi, la in the universal playground chant, "Na-na, na-na, na na na na na nah!"), lead a simple, silly call and response such as, "Today is Tuesday." They echo, "It is a blues day . . . A tiptoe-on-your-toes day . . . A chase-the-clouds-away day . . . A peanut-and-sing-along-sandwich day. . . ." Don't be afraid of being creative and spontaneous. If we had to plan every moment of our teaching day, we would never get any sleep. Make things up on the spur of the moment. Encourage creativity by setting up a creative environment; one in which you, the teacher, are creative.

Scat is a style of jazz singing in which the singer makes up either nonsense syllables or word phrases like "do be doo wah, zee doo-da zee dwah" or "What's that scat cat doing with the hat, Matt?" A simple way to teach scat singing to a class is to use the letters of the alphabet. You begin by asking for letters. Lisa suggests the letter *b*. You sing, "Ba ba ba biby baby bo." The class echoes. You sing, "Be bop ba boop bop bah!" The class echoes. You then assign letters to everyone in the class (avoid the letters *f* and *p* for obvious reasons). You then go around the room, asking each person to make up a scat phrase using their assigned letters, with everyone else repeating the phrase.

Another of many options is to have the singers sing sentences such as, "I don't know what to sing," "I wonder what's for lunch today," "I hear it's fish sticks," "Yucky ick ick!" The class repeats each phrase. Going around the room like this helps to build confidence in each singer, plus it's usually a lot of fun. Be careful. The wise guy/girl may want to throw in a negative statement. The best medicine in a case like this is preventive medicine. Tell students before you begin that there is no place for negativity in a creative classroom. If someone does do something negative, respond immediately.

Speaking of the wise guy/girl, when asked to repeat after the teacher, they will often play the game of repeating *everything* the teacher says, even phrases like "Ready?" You can prevent this by making up a visual symbol that means "repeat after me," or you can use a method that Kodály specialists use. Before singing each call and response song, sing, "Be my echo." Everyone repeats that and the teacher begins the song. This is clear, and it acts as an instant transition from a previous song (Choksy 1981).

You don't need to say, "Now we're going to sing a call and response song." Simply begin the song. This is true with most songs.

Another kind of call and response song is one in which the leader sings a phrase and the group sings a different phrase in response. Our first example is the South African Zulu prayer, "Thuma Mina, N'Kosia" (translation: Hear My Prayers, Oh Lord).

Thuma Mina, N'Kosia

A simple way to approach this song would be to teach the response parts only. When students have learned the responses and can sing them by themselves, then you can add your call part. Students need not know beforehand that there is a part other than their own. Telling them that could create confusion. Besides, it's a nice surprise when you come in with the lead part.

A similar call and response song is the civil rights song "Woke Up This Mornin'." It is based on the African American spiritual of the same name.

A simple way to teach this song is to present both parts to the group, using the rote system from chapter 5, then divide the group into two parts, practicing the lead, or call part with one group and the response part with the other, and finally putting the two parts together. Fix mistakes as you go along. Make sure that the two groups are physically separated from each

Woke Up This Mornin'
Civil Rights Version of Traditional Spiritual

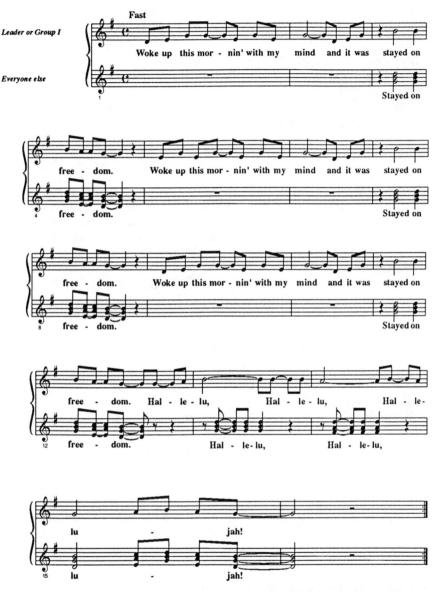

other. To make it more challenging, you can have the two groups switch parts, the call group becoming the response group and vice versa. As in many spirituals and civil rights songs, key words can be replaced. In this case "freedom" can be replaced with words such as "justice" or "liberty." Another option is to teach the lead part to your class, then have the audience at a school singing celebration learn and sing the response part.

Other great call and response songs in this style are the French song "Alouette" and the English song "The Keeper."

Call: Jacky Boy
Response: Master
Call: Sing ye well
Response: *Very well*
Call: Hey down
Response: *Ho Down*
Call: Derry derry down
Both: Among the leaves so green-o.

The collection of South African songs called *Freedom Is Coming* (see Appendix B) has many great call and response songs in this style. The song "Freedom Is Coming" appeals to all ages. I taught it to my seventh- and eighth-grade students who performed it for the school. The kindergarten students then wanted to learn it, but I told them it was too hard. They went out at recess and learned it from the junior high students. They came back to me and sang the song with both the call and the response parts. It was utterly charming.

This style of inexact call and response can be used beautifully in both white and black spirituals and gospel songs. For example, the spiritual "Swing Low Sweet Chariot" has a verse that goes like this:

Call: I looked over Jordan and what did I see?
Response: Comin' for to carry me home.

Call: A band of angels comin' after me.
Response: Comin' for to carry me home.

Both Groups: Swing low (swing low) sweet chariot,
  Comin' for to carry me home. (2x)

You won't always find spirituals and folk songs written out in the call and response style because they are part of the aural tradition. For those working within the folk music traditions, the printed song is simply the starting point for endless variations (see chapter 11.)

Teaching Songs Using Movements

Adding body movements and hand signs to songs is an amazingly effective way to teach songs both to children and to adults. It is especially effective when you are teaching songs with many words. The movement strategy is usually twice as effective as the rote method because it is multisensory. The more senses that are involved with learning, the faster the learning is (Gardner

1993, 5–34). The simple children's song "Head, Shoulders, Knees, And Toes" simply needs to be sung a few times with motions by the teacher in order for the students to learn it. As an example, let us use the following more challenging example:

Building Bridges

by the Women of Greenham Common Peace Encampment

Transcribed by Elizabeth Cave. Reprinted from *Rise Up Singing: The Group Singing Songbook*, by Peter Blood and Annie Patterson. Used by permission of the publisher, Sing Out Publications.

This song was written by the women of Greenham Common Peace Encampment in England in 1983. It is a song of solidarity for those who were protesting nuclear energy plants there. This is the tradition behind the song and should be discussed at some point in teaching the song.

For teaching the song, I use simple hand signs that give visual meaning to the words. These hand signs are not intended for use with hearing impaired people. This is an important point as many people in the hearing impaired community are sensitive about the token use of sign language, a language they have worked hard to make their own. They do not like seeing it trivialized. It is sometimes essential to explain that you are using hand signs only as a multisensory learning aid.

The first time through the song, I ask everyone to do the hand signs, but not to sing yet. Here are the signs I use. You can adapt them any way you wish, or you may create new ones.

Repeat the song doing the hand signs, telling students that the next time you want them to sing it with you. On the third time through, then, have them sing with you. They will still need about three more times through

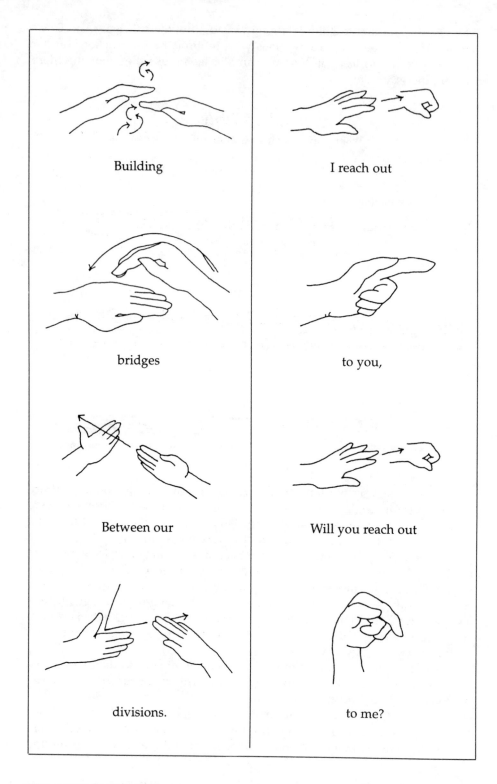

Building

I reach out

bridges

to you,

Between our

Will you reach out

divisions.

to me?

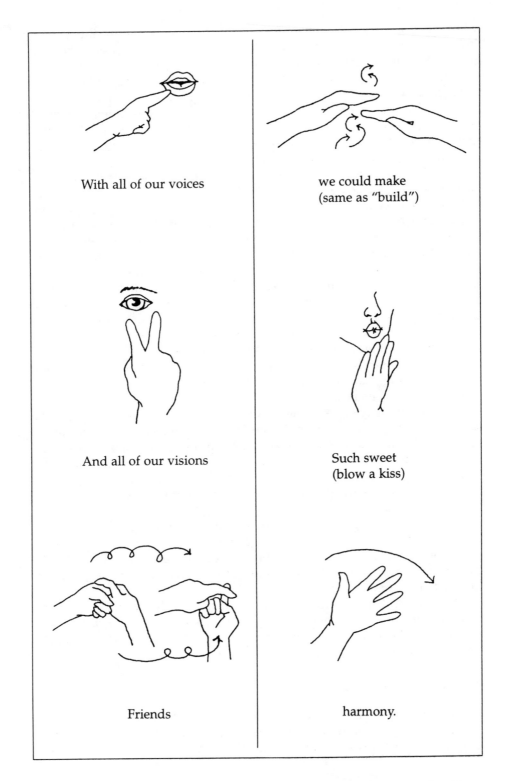

With all of our voices

we could make
(same as "build")

And all of our visions

Such sweet
(blow a kiss)

Friends

harmony.

before they can sing it by themselves. It can seem very dull to sing a song three times in a row, so each time I give them a new reason for singing it–even though the real reason I want them to do it again is so they can learn it through the process of repetition. For example, I might say, "This time, when you say, 'I reach out to you,' pretend to reach out to someone in the room." We sing it again. The next time I might say, "Now when you sing, such sweet harmony,' I want you to pretend to blow a kiss." We sing it again. These little tricks make the repetition fun.

Now the singers are almost ready to sing the whole song without you. They might have trouble with the last line, so you can reteach that line using the rote method. For some reason, the last lines of rounds are always the hardest to learn. Once the song can be sung without you singing along, you are ready for the next step. Even though the song is a round, I do not tell anyone. When they have learned it well enough so they can sing it by themselves, then I suddenly break up the class into two parts and do it in a round. (A round is a song like "Row, Row, Row Your Boat" that can be sung in layers with each group starting at different times.) I may not do "Building Bridges" as a round the first time I teach the song, but when it does happen, the reaction is one of awe, which is, after all, the reaction that we should seek every time. I then do it in four parts, which is even more amazing. Sing softly.

Why is teaching songs with body and hand motions so effective? Contrary to some assumptions, mind and body are not separate; they are connected. I believe that utilizing this connection is a natural and extremely effective way of enhancing learning.

There are many kinds of movement songs, and they do not need to be discussed in detail here. Generally speaking, movement songs teach themselves. Children pick up the melody and movement to a pattie cake song from watching and listening to it a few times. A song that requires dancing, such as the party song "Here We Go Looby Loo," can be danced right away by class members standing in a circle. As the song progresses, everyone will join in, "Put your right foot in and shake it all about."

Party game songs are very popular with children aged 3–8 precisely because they are games. Most of these games teach themselves because the movements that accompany them are so infectious and fun (Choksy 1981, 46–49; Jones and Hawes 1987; Rohrbough 1940, 1982; Langstaff and Langstaff 1978, 1986).

Important: Party game songs are great fun for the young child. Care must be taken, however, that the children sing in tune while they are having fun. If in-tune singing is somehow separated from fun singing, then ultimately the student is being taught to sing out of tune.

Storytelling with Songs

Storytellers have been combining songs and stories for millions of years. In many cultures, in fact, most stories are sung. Homer sang *The Iliad*. Praise singers in Western Africa chant stories to local leaders, telling of the leaders' many achievements and ridiculing the achievements of their rivals. The song lines of Australia are ancient paths on which elders "walk-about" singing creation stories and re-creating the world (Chatwin 1987).

Children love to sing and they love to hear stories. The combination of song and story can be very exciting, with children becoming very involved with the story. An excellent example of a song/story in print is Pete Seeger's adaptation of the South African song/story "Abiyoyo." This is the story of a magician who can make objects disappear and of his son who loves to sing a little song about a monster called "Abiyoyo." The song is sung throughout the story and eventually becomes integral to the story. Because the song is sung by the leader a few times first, by the time the students join in, they know it pretty well. The exciting thing about this story/song is that the monster attacks, and only by having everyone sing the song with energy can they make the monster dance and eventually lie down in exhaustion, thus giving the magician a chance to make Abiyoyo disappear. The combination of story and song are irresistible. The story, with song, has now been published with delightful illustrations (Seeger 1985).

Unfortunately, there are not many books that combine songs with stories like "Abiyoyo" so it is up to the creativity of the teacher to combine stories and songs. I have used the Native American chant "Wearing My Long Winged Feathers" to be used along with a story that also incorporates dance.

Wearing My Long Winged Feathers
Contemporary Native American

To perform this song/story, I choose and read an appropriate Native American creation story from a book (see *North American Native Authors Catalog*). At times, during the story, the class sings the song while one child dances like a bird around our seated circle. Other children act out the other parts.

You can add songs to your favorite stories. You can add stories to your favorite songs. The possibilities are endless.

In the whole language learning environment, the combination of stories and songs can be very valuable, particularly if word recognition is also incorporated. Illustrated signs with key words on them can be used to help tell the story.

Many songs are stories in themselves and can be adapted to become song/stories. Examples are songs like "The Fox," "Froggie Went a-Courtin'," "Aunt Rhody," the Beatles' "Yellow Submarine," and Tom Paxton's delightful "Going to the Zoo."

Another example of the creative use of a song/story was demonstrated by a kindergarten teacher friend of mine, Kathy Fiveash. Kathy was doing a unit on dinosaurs with her class, and she adapted the folk song "Children Go Where I Send Thee," replacing "Four was the four that stood at the door" with references to different dinosaurs doing silly things. "The tyrannosaur that stood at the door." The class then illustrated posters, each with the name of a dinosaur, one for each verse.

When I taught "Thula Klizeo" in chapter 6, I told the story behind the song. The words to songs say, "Be still my heart, even here I am at home." As a reminder, I told of the ancient Zulu tradition of dancing with amazing kicks in the air and majestic stomps to the earth. I told of how the South African government then forbid the Zulu people from expressing any pride through traditional dances or songs and of how the Zulus then created the modern tradition called "Es-kah'-tah-mee-yah," to stomp quietly, to show their pride and power in a way that would not get them locked up in jail. This story must be told when the song is sung. By accompanying songs with the stories behind them you create the roots to the tree, the foundation upon which the song can then bloom. Chapter 10 discusses this in greater detail.

Singing Rounds

Rounds and canons are wonderful to sing. They require participants to listen very carefully while singing, and anything that makes us listen is beneficial, both musically and academically. There is no single strategy for teaching rounds, but there are some simple guidelines.

Teach each round using the strategy that best fits the song. A round like "Hey Ho Nobody Home," for example, would best be taught using the simple rote method in which students repeat one line at a time, eventually putting the whole song together.

It is essential that the class ultimately be able to sing the song well without your singing along or without accompaniment. If singers still need such a crutch, they will always want to sing only what you are singing or playing. They must be able to sing the round by themselves before you break the class up into sections for the round.

A moment ago I mentioned a simple round teaching trick that I learned

Hey Ho Nobody Home   Trad. Round

from composer Alice Parker (Parker 1986). Teach the song without telling them it's a round. They're singing the song through a few times when you suddenly turn it into a round. You don't even say anything. Simply signal one side of the class to be silent, while cueing the second side to begin the round again. Don't break between repetitions.

Here are some more tips for leading rounds:

- Have everyone sing softly so they can hear the other parts. The second most common mistake when singing rounds (after trying to sing a song as a round before it can be sung in unison) is to sing loudly. When we sing loudly, we cannot hear the other parts, we end up going too fast or too slow, and the combined sound ends up being competitive rather than cooperative. Have students sing softly and listen when they sing rounds. We should sing with our ears, not our voices.
- It is important to position your strong singers when you divide the class up into parts for a round. Don't have all the strong singers on one side.
- Always teach the last line of a round carefully. It is often the hardest line to remember. When singing a round, practice singing the round a few times through in unison so everyone knows when to repeat the beginning. Cue each group to repeat after they are done. Once students have sung a round well in two parts, go on to more parts if possible.
- Some rounds end well when you have everyone stop at the same time, although they are all singing different lines at the time. Group one will be singing the third phrase; group two, the second; and group three, the first. Give them a clear sign that you are ending. They all end at the same time. Individual endings may have to be rehearsed. A much easier way to end a round is to have each group stop after their last line, one group at a time. Each group will need to be cued to stop. This can be tricky for you, as it requires you to pay attention as to where each group is. The type of ending you use depends on

the song itself. Canons are often composed to end together, with rounds ending one group at a time, but this is not a standard rule.

- If you are teaching a song and you find that the singers can't do it in a round yet, don't quit and leave everyone feeling frustrated as they may not want to sing it the next time. Have students sing the song once again in unison so that everyone feels confident about it, then explain that the next time they sing it, they will try to do it as a round.

The Zipper Song

A zipper song is a song in which most of the verse remains the same, with one or more words being substituted each time "This Old Man" is a classic zipper song.

> This old man, he played <u>one</u>,
> he played knick-knack on my <u>thumb</u>,
> With a knick-knack paddy-wack, give your dog a bone.
> This old man came rolling home.

The underlined words are then replaced with "two . . . on my shoe," "three . . . on my knee," "four . . . door," "five . . . hive," "six . . . sticks," "seven . . . up in heaven," "eight . . . on my plate," "nine . . . on my spine," "ten . . . once again." Other children's zipper songs are "Old McDonald" and "She'll Be Comin' Round The Mountain."

Some African American hymns follow the zipper song form, although the noble beauty of the hymns defy the informality of the term "zipper." Examples are "Over My head," "Cumbayah," and "There Is More Love Somewhere."

Teach this song phrase by phrase using the rote method. Teach the third line in two sections because it is tricky. Once they have learned the song, begin substituting words, "There is more joy" or "peace" or "hope." Ask singers to provide one syllable words. Do not trivialize the cultural tradition of the song by adding nonsense words. It is a dignified song. There are plenty of other songs to have fun with.

Zipper songs are great sing-along songs because they require little learning time and can be sung for a long time. An audience during an assembly can pick up on a zipper song and join in.

The Nonstrategy

I have discussed many strategies for teaching songs, but I have left out one of the most common strategies, the one I call the nonstrategy. I don't know what else to call it, because it literally means teaching a song without any strategy. How is this done? Simple. Sing any song slowly and ask everyone

There Is More Love Somewhere

Traditional African American

There is more love some - where. There is more love
peace peace

some - where. I'm gon-na Keep on 'till I find it,

There is more love some - where. There is
peace

to sing with you simultaneously. Every syllable and vowel are a hair late, but the song gets sung. With enough repetitions, the song is learned.

I do not recommend the nonstrategy for most songs, but there will certainly be times when it will be perfectly appropriate, particularly when good singing is not your goal and you simply want to play and have some fun; an admirable goal.

Many songs simply teach themselves because of their simplicity. The joyful repetition in the classic spiritual "This Little Light of Mine" defies teaching. People simply learn it from hearing it.

> This little light of mine, I'm gonna' let it shine. (3x)
> Let it shine, Let it shine, Let it shine.
>
> Everywhere I go, I'm gonna let it shine. (3x)
> Let it shine, Let it shine, Let it shine.

Additional verses: All around the town . . . Building a new world . . . Free of fear and hatred . . . Sing a song of freedom . . . Sing a song of justice . . . All around this world . . . Life is like a circle . . . I believe in music . . . The harmony of voices . . . Our voices sing together . . .

You and your singers can make up a million more verses. Return to the top of the first verse, "This little light of mine," once in a while. If you want, make other changes as you go along. Sing some verses fast, some slow, some loud, some soft. Sing some verses as a blues or a lullaby or a rock or rap song. If you're going to "let it shine," this sometimes means shining with creativity.

The song teaching strategies again are as follows:

The rote method
Call and response
Hand signs/movement/dance
The story strategy
Rounds
The zipper song
The nonstrategy

Choose your song. Decide on the best strategy. Practice teaching the song to a mirror or a colleague before you teach it to a class.

I have tried to make all this sound easy, but song teaching is like any other kind of teaching: It takes practice. You have to be prepared—know the song, know the strategy, be prepared to fix mistakes. You should even be prepared to switch strategies midsong.

Once you've taught a few songs in each strategy, it will become easy. The challenge will then become making everyone sound great, in tune, and full of life. And that is what the next chapters are about.

Sing and shine on.

Everyone Can
Sound Beautiful

· · · · · · · · · · · · · · · · · · · Do you ever cry with joy when you hear children sing? Does the sound of children's voices ever give you goose bumps and fill you with awe? Or do children's voices sound cute but flawed—like immature versions of adults?

We don't appreciate children enough if we experience their voices in the latter manner. Children are magnificent in every sense, and their voices have the same capacity to create wonder and awe as adult voices, maybe even more so. In a child's voice, there is a purity of sound and an unblocked emotional quality that can be truly spellbinding. Expect miracles. How?

First, teach children to sing in tune by having them sing songs that they *can* sing in tune and by constantly insisting that they use the "inner hearing" technique to be discussed in chapter 9. All this should happen, of course, in a fully supportive classroom—one in which praise, not mockery, is used by students and teachers alike. Second, allow the children to be in awe of their own voices. Do this by having children sing awe-inspiring music—music steeped in tradition and meaning—and by insisting that the children sound amazing at all times. How?

I suggest a playful variation of a voice exercise practiced by the Chicago Children's Choir where I worked as training units director and conductor. Bang! You may already be thinking, "Voice exercises? This is way over my head!" Let's not think of these as exercises, but as games or activities. They are, as you will see, fun, and they make a world of difference in children's singing. These techniques can also be used with adults.

Singing with Resonance

In Part 1 of this book, I discussed resonance. As a reminder, resonance is a fancy word for sound. It refers to sound waves that vibrate or resonate. I also spoke of overtones or harmonics. These are the higher sounds created by singing or playing an instrument. They give tonal color to sound. When you combine the primary colors red and yellow, you get green. Similarly, the colors of sound are affected by adding or taking away overtones. As a reminder, if you were to take away the overtones, the basic sound of a violin and a flute would be the same. What makes these instruments sound so different are the overtones that each instrument creates. The human voice also creates these overtones. We each create different overtones, which is one reason each of our voices is different.

Each voice has a whole spectrum of possible tones–from a whispered breathiness to an irritating nasality, and from a high screech to a harsh rasp. All unhealthy tones should be avoided. This is common sense. If a tone sounds as if it might hurt a singer's voice, it probably will.

In a playful way, I teach children to create four different tones. They don't need to know anything about overtones to do this. I simply choose a song they know, for example, the round "Row, Row, Row Your Boat." I then lead the following activities:

- Tone One: First I have the children sing the song with as much breathiness as they can. I call this the cute, breathy tone. I ask them if they notice that they have to breathe a lot more when they sing with breathy voices. As a challenge, I sometimes ask them to sing a whole phrase of "Row, Row, Row Your Boat" without breathing. Usually they don't get past the word "boat."
- Tone Two: Then I ask the children to sing the song as if they were opera singers with big, thick voices. This is usually abetted by having them sit up, lift their heads, and make noble operatic gestures with their hands. I call this the grand voice. It's okay if the children giggle through this—they're playing with their voices, perhaps for the first time.
- Tone Three: Now comes the children's favorite tone—the ugly, nasal tone. I ask the children to pinch their noses with their fingers. Then I ask them to sing "Row, Row, Row your Boat," or whatever song they are singing, with as much nasality as they can. There are usually lots of laughs accompanying this "exercise." I often ask the children to do it again, but louder. It is extremely important that they do not resort to yelling or raspy singing as both can damage the throat. Identify unhealthy singing if you hear the children doing it. The nasal sound should come from their noses, not their throats. See if

the children can sing with a nasal tone without pinching their noses.

At this point, I review all three tones. You may even go one step further and have the children switch tones in the middle of the song. Help them do this by calling out the tone that you want as they sing. Children love this.

- Tone Four: I then explain to the children, in perfect seriousness, that I don't want them to sing any of the previous three tones. I tell them that what I want is called the big, beautiful voice. What I don't tell them is that the sound I want is a combination of the previous three tones, with an emphasis on the ugly, nasal tone. Have them sing "Row, Row, Row Your Boat" with their new big and beautiful voices. The wonderful results will be well worth the effort.

Before you try these tone activities with your students, you may wish to do some experimenting yourself. Try singing a song of your choice in your natural voice. As you sing, listen very carefully—listen for the breathiness. It's there. Listen for the nasality. It too is there. Listen for the grand operatic sound. Now sing again and add more breathiness, or add more nasality, or add more of the grand tone. Play around with these for a while. Really concentrate on listening to yourself. Experiment with the placement of your tongue—forward, back, low, high. Lift your eyebrows. Lifting your eyebrows lifts the palate of your mouth that brightens your sound. Sing with your arms straight up in the air. How does this change the sound? It affects your breathing and strengthens your voice.

Most of us are not aware of the overtones in our voices. I wasn't, until I spent a week chanting and toning with sound healer and educator Don Campbell. By listening to my voice sing one vowel for a long time, I gradually became very aware of the overtones, the higher tones that ring quietly above our regular voice. We often have to learn or relearn how to listen.

Once you have experimented for a while, work on the big beautiful voice. Sing one tone, not too high or too low, on the oh sound. As you sing, add a touch of nasality. It's a lot like mixing colors when painting. I like to emphasize the nasal sound so that I can get my voice to ring without sounding too nasal. All voices are different, so you will have to find what is most comfortable for you.

When you do this exercise, the nasal tone brings out the overtones that I mentioned earlier. Overtones are good for vocalizing; they make your voice distinctive. Public speakers who use lots of overtones when speaking tend to keep their audiences awake. They are speaking with resonance. Speakers with muddy voices, low in overtones, can put listeners to sleep (Campbell 1989, 47–48).

At the end of this chapter, I've included a brief extension to these singing techniques—one that is a bit more advanced, but simple to understand.

Once you know how to create your own big, beautiful sound, try doing it with your students. Your voice can now be the model for their voices. Ask them to imitate your tone. Make it a playful activity. Sing another song, switching between the four tones as you sing through it. Ask for more nasality until you get just the sound you want. Identify that sound as the big, beautiful tone.

When children sing with the big, beautiful tone, with enough nasality to make the tone ring, a truly beautiful sound is created. When children hear themselves singing this way it often creates the reaction of awe, "Wow! We sound good!"

Every time you sit down to sing with your students, play around with the different tones, particularly the nasal tone. In time, the big, beautiful tone will become very natural. It does take time, though.

Note that if you feel uncomfortable using your voice as a model for the students, do not despair. You can use the students' own voices as models. In order for this to work, however, the students must feel comfortable singing by themselves. To facilitate this, go around the room and have everyone sing, one at a time. This will build the students' confidence. Then use the voice of one student as a model for the other students. Don't use the same student repeatedly, however; give different students chances to be the model.

As you teach children to sing well, keep in mind that good posture is essential for great singing. Whether sitting or standing, singers' backs should be naturally straight, and both their feet should be flat on the ground. I was once told by a Native American healer from Ohio that one should always sing with one's feet on the ground. To paraphrase him, "When your feet are on the ground, you are connected to the Earth; when you are connected to the Earth, you are connected with the power of the Earth; when you are connected to the power of the Earth, you can sing with the power of the Earth. Always sing with the power of the Earth." I have taught this to children. It is a strong metaphor with a great deal of truth in it.

Movement and Other Exercises

Teach children to sing with their bodies as well as their emotions and their minds. When the body is brought into singing, the improvement can be amazing. Do a simple exercise to demonstrate to children that the whole body is responsive to sound and music—that the whole body hears. Ask everyone to stretch their arms and freely yawn with lots of sound. Then have them stretch without making any sound at all. Ask them if the silent stretch feels as good as the stretch *with* sound. It doesn't. Help children understand that when they sing, they are giving themselves a sound massage, both inside and out. You can easily make resonant yawning and stretching part of your singing repertoire.

Dance and move when you sing. Jump in the air. Walk around the room. March. Play pattie cake. Massage each other's backs. Shake hands. Hug. Roll on the floor. Become singing bears, walking on all fours. Bounce, singing as you go.

It is important to remember that in most world cultures, singing is not a stationary activity. When one sings, one moves. Singing and moving are a natural combination, and these two activities strengthen each other.

Play *isolation* games. In these games, you try to concentrate on one isolated activity while simultaneously doing a completely different activity. For example, have the children concentrate on singing "Twinkle, Twinkle Little Star" while simultaneously imitating face motions that you make. Grimace, frown, laugh, cry; show fear, surprise, worry, love, hate. Tell the children that they must not let the sound of the song change when they change their facial expressions. Then have the children move around the room while singing the song. Shout out the name of an emotion. Have the children show emotions like fear, hate, or love in their bodies, again without changing the sound of the song. Shout out the name of an animal. Have the students imitate that animal while singing the song as naturally as they can. This is lots of fun and is very good for the children as the act of isolating one activity is excellent for their ability to concentrate.

One goal of this chapter has been to illustrate that children can sing beautifully. They can learn to sing with resonance. They can sing with the big, beautiful tone. In the first part of the book, I spoke of how sound charges the brain. But not all sounds charge the brain in the same way. Some sounds, such as dull and breathy tones, can actually have a negative effect on the brain's activities (Gilmor 1989, 210). Full, resonant tones, on the other hand, create a dynamo of energy for the brain. When children are encouraged to sing with resonance, many wonderful things happen. Not only are their brains charged, but their spirits and bodies are charged as well. Their sense of awe and self-worth is charged, and their desire to sing, to move, to learn, and to be alive is charged. This may sound like a preposterous promise, but I have seen it happen over and over again. Singing with a resonant tone creates energy.

Optional Vocal Exercises

What follows is information on some additional experiments that you can do with your own voice so that you can use it as a model for your students. If you feel that you have had enough information on tone, however, go on to another chapter, particularly chapter 9 on singing in tune.

Try some experimenting with these four sounds: ah, oh, ee, and oo. Sing each on a single pitch. As you sing, notice the changes you have to make in the shape of your mouth. Your mouth and lips are open wide for the ah. To make the ee sound, you have to almost make a wide smile. For the oo, you do a slight pucker of the lips. The oh is like a combination of ah and oo, with mouth open, but lips puckered slightly. Play around with these shapes for a while, seeing how changes in the tongue, jaw, and lips affect the vowels.

Now try these:

- Sing the ah sound with a cute, breathy tone.
- Sing the oh sound with a grand operatic tone.
- Sing the ee sound with an ugly, nasal tone.
- Sing the oo sound with a big, beautiful tone.

Now experiment with the colors of your voice. As you are singing the ah sound with a cute, breathy tone, add a touch of the oh sound with the grand, operatic tone. Keep the ah sound going while you change the shape of your mouth.

Now sing the ah sound, adding a touch of the ee sound with a nasal tone. Then do both the ah and oo. Go through each of the four sounds, adding the other sounds one at a time. Play with this as you did before. What these exercises do is to remind you of the importance of shaping the jaw, mouth, and lips.

Final note: You may apply all this tone quality information to your classroom singing, and the students may still sound dull and lifeless. If this is the case, doing more work with their tone probably will not help. Moving will. Another solution is to make the rhythm of the song more exciting. Tell the students to imagine hitting a drum with a drumstick. Then ask them to imagine that every consonant is a percussive sound, like hitting the drum. Demonstrate this for them. It is amazing what a difference this simple technique can make on singing. It energizes it. I learned this from singing black gospel music, in which even the slowest songs are often sung with a percussive edge.

This technique of asking the students to imagine hitting a drum with their voices is an example of guided imagery. Guided imagery is most often used as a meditation and/or therapy technique. The leader of a group asks everyone to feel, see, taste, or hear the images he or she is describing. Our brains are capable of imagining just about anything. Guided imagery can be used in teaching music as a replacement to long explanations. For example, I could ask students to sing with nasal tones in their low registers on a medium loud note, or I could ask them to sing like goats. The latter request will work much better and will be more fun.

Always make singing fun and have fun with it yourself.

9

Everyone Can Sing in Tune

LARRY AND Paula were both ten-year-olds who had sung out of tune before I met them. They are now fine singers due to the simple techniques that I used—techniques that any teacher can learn.

We are all different, with unique strengths and weaknesses. Some of us can shoot baskets with ease. Others have great difficulty with this. The same is true with music, and no one should ever deny it. Dealing with strengths and weaknesses is something we have to do all our lives, but just because we are weak in an area does not mean that we are untalented or incapable of excelling in this area. With singing, it takes a constant determination on the part of both teacher and student for the student to sing well. But it *can* be done. We can do it. I have seen it happen thousands of times with people of all ages.

The New York–based song leader and composer Alice Parker has a wonderful saying: "In music, you get exactly what you ask for, and no more." This is certainly true of in-tune singing.

It is an incorrect assumption that singing out of tune is natural and un-correctable. The out-of-tune child is more or less ignored, often delegated to play percussion instead of singing. Fortunately, music specialists have become more sensitive to this and are less likely to say, "Please mouth the words."

Why We Sing Out of Tune

The vocal cords are muscles in the throat that produce the sounds. Air from the lungs is set into vibration by the vocal cords, then amplified in the nasal

87

cavities and mouth. The tongue, palate, teeth, and lips help shape the sound, adding consonants, refining the vowels, and with the nasal cavities, creating the overtones. The healthy larynx is capable of a great range of pitches from low to high sounds, sometimes as many as five octaves. Like all muscles, however, there may be strong and weak points. Some people may never use their high voices. The muscles in the larynx required to create those high sounds may be weak. They will have difficulty singing high notes. The same can be true of low notes or even of medium notes.

Sometimes there is tension in the neck and larynx that inhibits the singing. Simple relaxation activities like vocal yawning and stretching can be beneficial. Be sure that the students make lots of healthy sounds as they yawn. Combine the yawn and siren exercises. Gradually every singer will obtain a healthy voice, but this is only part of the solution to out-of-tune singing. We still haven't explained the principle reason why people sing out of tune.

Once upon a time, it was acceptable to blame the voice alone for all out-of-tune singing, but this is no longer the case. It is the ear that determines pitch. To sing a note in tune, we must first be able to hear the note in our head. When we hear that note, we can then reproduce it with our vocal chords. Until we can truly hear a note correctly, we cannot sing it correctly. It's that simple.

Like the vocal chords, there are strong and weak parts of the ear. We may hear higher sounds better than lower or the lower sounds will be heard perfectly, but not the higher. Sometimes there may be gaps in our hearing. We might be able to hear low, medium, and high sounds, with the exception of four or five consecutive notes in the medium high range. Each ear is different. Each may have its own weaknesses and strengths. A sound that we hear in one ear may not be heard in another. Usually one ear is stronger than the other. In most cases if you are right-handed, your right ear will be the dominant ear, and vice versa. Sometimes we may do damage to our ears. There are many things that can go wrong, but the principal problem remains: If you can't hear a note correctly, then you can't sing it correctly.

Some specialists believe that if the mother does not sing to the child, or if she sings out of tune, the child will not learn to listen correctly. Others blame crib toys that make music that is out of tune. It is my belief that people sing out of tune simply because they make the assumption that if you *don't* sing in tune, then you *can't* sing in tune. This is not so.

The ears of most younger children do not fully mature until puberty. This means that at a young age, there are still some notes the child will not hear accurately. We use the word *range* to describe the area between two notes. The ideal range for a five-year-old to sing is between middle C and the G. The child has an ideal range of five notes, a fifth. Almost all five-year-olds hear those notes well.

If half the students in a kindergarten class can sing well, but only within a range of the five notes above middle C, then singing songs with much larger ranges would be a disservice to these children. Singing songs that have pitches above or below children's ideal ranges may cause them to sing out of tune. Since they are not yet able to hear or to sing these higher or lower pitches, they may end up singing wrong notes instead. By doing songs with wide ranges, a teacher may actually be teaching children to sing out of tune. For example, the song "Somewhere Over the Rainbow" is loved by children, but its range is very large—eight notes. If that song is taught by the well-meaning kindergarten teacher, it is likely that half the class will sing it out of tune.

The obvious solution for this problem is to only sing songs with small ranges—songs like "Twinkle Twinkle Little Star" or the South African song discussed in chapter 6, "Thula Klizeo." More on this in a moment.

Someone who sings in tune is said to have *good intonation*. The meaning of intonation is easy to remember. Simply keep in mind that one of the goals of powerful singing is to have a nation of in-tune singers—in other words, an "in-tune-nation."

Singing in tune can become a problem for many boys who sing in tune during their early years, but who become confused when they reach puberty. When their voices change, they have difficulty matching their new voices with what they hear.

I have worked with many adult men who had stopped singing when their voices changed. They had gone for many years thinking they had poor intonation. Actually, they simply hadn't made the necessary step of retraining their ears and voices. These men can quickly learn to sing in tune.

When each of us sings, we create soft overtones or pitches above our main pitch. If we could hear all of these overtones, the loudest ones would form what is called a major chord—the first, third, and fifth notes of the scale. Often, the out-of-tune person will hear the overtones instead of the main pitch, which is why many out-of-tune people sing their notes either a third or a fifth higher than they should (or a fourth lower, which, technically speaking, is the same as a fifth higher). (When we say "a fifth higher" it simply means five notes higher, counting the principle pitch as one. A fifth higher than A would be E.)

Why We Need to Sing in Tune

Larry and Paula, the two students who sang out of tune, were considered untalented by those around them. Larry's father told me in confidence that his son had inherited his inability to do music. If we were to ask our students whether they were talented, we might be surprised at how many would say that they were not. This is all part of a general pattern in which we perceive a huge separation between talented and untalented people. As stated in the first part of this book, most cultures do not have this separation; in more cultures everyone is considered talented and capable of making wonderful music.

Tone deafness is a convenient invention of a pass/fail system—either you can sing or you can't, goes the argument. Tone deafness is one of the many excuses we use to deny ourselves the power of music. Some of these excuses are as follows: "I'm a lousy singer," "I can't carry a tune," "I have no voice," "I'm not musical," "I can't read music, so why sing?" "Girls sing, boys don't," "I don't have an ear for music," "Music is for talented people only," and, the worst of them all, "My teacher told me to mouth the words."

I travel around a great deal leading sing-alongs. Everywhere I go I ask for so-called tone deaf people to come up and be cured or to see me afterward. With the many people who have challenged me, I have not yet met a person I couldn't teach to sing in tune. This may mean that I teach a so-called tone deaf person to match only one or two pitches, but those pitches can be the starting points on a journey of recovery, which can be very exciting. Once people discover that they can sing in tune, after years of thinking otherwise, they can gradually improve their intonation. I give them some tips on things to work on (more on these in a moment). If the person is determined to sing in tune, he or she can do it. You are reteaching the ear how to listen. Like all learning activities, it takes time.

In terms of Larry and Paula, they were both fine students. There was no reason why they should be labeled poor singers simply because they had very minor problems with their listening. There was also no reason why they and the other students in the class couldn't share in the full power of group singing—something that could not happen unless the majority of the class was singing in tune. For example, if twenty-five children sing a song, with a third of the class singing out of tune, it will not be as powerful an experience. Whereas, if the class can sing the song and sound great doing so, the pride alone will fill the students with excitement and a strong sense of positive self-worth.

There is an added benefit to singing in tune, one that may seem highly technical, but which is very fundamental to understanding music. As I have mentioned, every single sound is actually made up of many different sounds or harmonics at the same time. All except the lowest harmonics are very faint; in fact, the lowest sound is so much louder you probably won't hear the higher notes at first. But they are there. When many voices are gathered together, something special happens with these harmonics. They begin to ring like chimes. Twenty-five voices suddenly sound like a thousand. The room is filled with resonance. It is a powerful experience, impossible to explain with words. If the voices are out of tune, however, the resulting tone will be muddy and unclear. It will certainly have no excitement to it. The in-tune sound, particularly when sung by children, is a miraculous sound, truly awe inspiring. When children hear their combined voices, not only are they filled with pride, but they are filled with awe, wonder, and a powerful sense of being alive.

How to Create the Positive Atmosphere

The first step I used in Larry and Paula's class was to create a classroom atmosphere that was fully supportive of every student. As part of the supportive environment, I constantly reminded the students how wonderful they sounded. Mistakes were welcome, but ridicule of someone else's mistake was not. Both teachers and students had to support one another. If Larry or Paula had felt attacked, even in the most subtle way, they most likely would have given up emotionally. I had to be constantly on my guard; unsupportive behavior had to be challenged immediately by me. Using the techniques I will soon outline, I taught the class to sing in tune. It didn't happen overnight, but it did happen.

I stressed the positive so much with this class, in fact, that I often asked for standing ovations when the students sang well. This created a harmless and playful atmosphere in which forms of punishment were unnecessary. Our friends Larry and Paula saw that the process of singing well wasn't such a big deal, certainly no life and death issue. And, because they got the support of their fellow students, it became all the more powerful an experience for them.

If the school where you teach gives grades, designate a category in smiling, so that along with other marks on the report card, a student can receive an A for smiling. It's silly, of course, but it helps to create a positive atmosphere. I taught at Wheelock College in Boston for several years. My former students can testify that they got extra credit for smiling.

I am often asked if I ever work with out-of-tune children in private. The answer is no because I am very confident that they can improve quite well in class through getting the peer support that they need. When you teach in-tune singing for the first time, however, you may want to work privately with individual students until you are confident with the techniques. If a student does not do well in front of her or his peers and does not receive support, there may be little motivation to continue. Students must always do well and must always receive support, such as the thrill of receiving a standing ovation. Doing well may simply mean matching one pitch correctly, but they must understand that they did well.

Too many times, out-of-tune singing is seen as a problem that should be kept secret. To bring a child's singing problem out in the open is seen as potentially discouraging for the child. By not acknowledging the problem, it is hoped that everyone's life will go on smoothly. What actually happens is that both in-tune and out-of-tune students receive the hidden message that if they have a problem of any kind, it should be kept secret. This is not a good message. If the class were a family, psychologists would call the class dysfunctional.

In my classrooms, I have always tried to create supportive environments in which children with intonation problems can learn to sing in tune. A truly supportive environment is one in which all students know and feel in their hearts that, if they have a problem, no matter what it is, it can be worked on and, hopefully, solved. As I have said, there are no huge gaps between the talented and the untalented. We are all pretty amazing.

If a student, for whatever reason, never learns to sing in tune, he or she certainly should not be punished. Our emphasis is on joyful singing. I do not advocate a rigid approach wherein a student may feel inadequate for not singing in tune. I simply believe that if hearing people can sing in tune, every effort should be made to teach them how. This is only possible in a truly supportive environment, one in which the talent of every student is recognized.

How to Find the Right Range

As I said previously, the most important thing to understand when teaching a class to sing in tune is that songs with small ranges will sound better than songs with big ranges. If there are six notes that the class sounds good singing, then find songs that use those six notes. "Twinkle Twinkle Little Star" is a great song with a range of six notes.

```
C       D       E       F       G       A       B       C
1       2       3       4       5       6       7       8
```

A scale is a sequence of eight consecutive notes with the first and last note being the same (C-D-E-F-G-A-B-C.) Musicians worldwide use what are called solfège syllables to spell out the scale (do-re-mi-fa-sol-la-ti-do as in the song "Doe, a Deer" from *The Sound of Music*). Instead of using either of those systems, we will use numbers (1-2-3-4-5-6-7-8). Numbers help to remind us of ranges—it is a convenient measuring system. If I were to sing "Twinkle Twinkle Little Star" using the eight numbers from the scale, it would be:

```
1  1  5  5  6  6  5—,  4  4  3  3  2  2  1—,
5  5  4  4  3  3  2—,  5  5  4  4  3  3  2—,
1  1  5  5  6  6  5—,  4  4  3  3  2  2  1—.
```

The next step is to choose the right range, not too high and not too low. If the first note is on middle C, it will be in a good range for children.

Some songs may have only one or two notes that go high or low. For example, the South African song from chapter 6 has one high note that sticks out. All the rest of the notes are in a small range and are therefore easy to sing in tune. It is okay to sing songs that have occasional high or low notes. It would be very difficult, in fact, to find only songs with small ranges. This is especially true since most adults who write songs for young children use adult ranges because they make the false assumption that all young children can sing the same ranges as adults.

Songs written by children for children are always the best songs to sing for improving intonation. Have you ever heard jump-rope songs sung out of tune? No. Why? Because songs written by children for children usually have small ranges. The songs also have lots of repetition, something that helps intonation for the obvious reason that learning any skill requires repetition.

If all that I have said seems too specialized, please do not despair. The techniques for teaching in-tune singing can be used by anyone, with or without understanding the theories behind them.

The Steps in Teaching Students to Sing in Tune

In order for Larry and Paula to sing in tune, they first had to learn to hear the notes correctly. I used the simple technique called *inner hearing*, which simply means hearing a note inside one's head. With this technique, instead of asking students to immediately match a given pitch, you first ask them to hear it inside their heads. Once they hear it, you ask them to repeat it. If they can hear the note inside their heads using the following guidelines, then it is impossible for them not to sing it correctly.

Here, in greater detail are the steps I use:

1. Create a positive environment as previously discussed. Do these exercises with the entire class. You don't need to single out any students.

2. Find a note that is in a comfortable range, such as E above middle C. Sing the note on an *oo* sound.

Why oo? I mentioned before that out-of-tune people often hear the harmonics rather than the main pitch. The oo sound has the least number of overtones in it; it is therefore the best vowel to use for matching pitches.

3. Have students listen to the note in their heads. Ask them if they can hear the note inside their heads. The response will usually be "Yes," because we are conditioned to say "Yes" to such questions. Ask again, "Can you *really* hear the note?"

4. Once you are confident that the students can hear the note inside their heads, smile and ask them to sing it back to you. They will. Congratulate them. Give lots of support.

5. If some children do not match the note the first time around, try it again. Singing a slightly lower pitch usually helps. Ask for silence in the class. If there are any distracting hums from electrical appliances (usually B-flat in North America), turn them off. If the atmosphere is negative, fear and frustration will become overbearing for some students, which is why support is so essential. When you try it the second time, children will usually get the note right. I usually don't work with individual students until around the third grade. Until then I simply work with the entire class.

Sometimes your voice may not be suited as a model for the students to echo. For example, if I, as a man with a low voice, ask children to hear my pitch, some children might be thrown off. In time, students can adjust to my voice, but until then I use the simple technique of asking a student in the class to sing the note I want reproduced by the rest of the class or by the individual who is having intonation difficulties.

The individual who is having trouble matching pitches may have a lower voice than others. You would want that student to match a lower pitch. A simple, though not always accurate, way to determine whether a child's singing voice is high or low, is to listen to the child's speaking voice. A low speaking voice often indicates a low singing voice and vice versa.

If a child is still singing out of tune, find out if that child is right- or left-handed. Their dominant hand will be their dominant ear, so if they are right-handed, stand by their right ear and ask them to hear the note you will sing. Then have them sing it. It's amazing how effective this little technique is. Without anyone suspecting what you are doing, you can seat an in-tune singer by the right side of the right-handed out-of-tune singer. This will be an enormous help.

6. Go through steps two through four again, but now on a new note—again not too high or too low. Don't forget to smile.

7. Next, sing two consecutive notes. The ideal pitches are *sol* and *mi*, a descending minor third; the fifth and third notes of the scale. These are the pitches young children sing in their playground games such as in the taunting chant, "Na na, na na, nana nana na na!" No child has ever sung this ancient melody out of tune. It is impossible to do.

8. Continue this process over many classes, eventually adding more notes. Don't try to do all of the steps at once. Work on the steps gradually, making advances each time.

I learned a great technique while working in the Chicago public schools: The students would be seated in a semicircle. I would ask each student to sing by him or herself during each class. This may have meant singing one or two pitches or singing a short phrase such as the first two words of "The Star Spangled Banner," "Oh say . . ." Going around to every student kept them on their toes, and it gave me a chance to check their progress. Constant singing in this way makes students' confidence grow tremendously. Again, I wouldn't single out students in the lower grades.

I found that if I gave the students little singing goals to work on, they would take it very seriously, whether that goal was getting more breath, sitting up straight, or singing with more resonance (less breathy).

9. As the children become more and more secure in their intona-tion, begin singing songs with more difficult ranges. For example, you could now sing "Doe, a Deer" from *The Sound of Music* or "Somewhere Over the Rainbow" from *The Wizard of Oz*. These songs use all eight notes of the scale.

Singing rounds is excellent for intonation because it requires a more advanced kind of listening. Singers must listen to two or more interdependent parts at the same time. Any advancement in listening is an advancement in intonation.

10. Encourage children to use their higher voices (E up to C'). The technical term for this part of the vocal range is the *head voice*. Using the head voice, as opposed to the lower chest voice, is better for good intonation. This may mean that you, the teacher, may have to sing in a range higher than you are comfortable with, but this is necessary if you want your students to have good intonation.

Sometimes out-of-tune students can't hear the notes they are asked to sing because they are singing so loudly that they cease to hear anything well at all. Simply ask them to sing softer and concentrate on listening to their voices.

11. I have one last intonation technique to share, and this is probably the most important of all. Don't use any instruments to accompany the singing. This is called a cappella singing. A cappella singing is best suited for intonation work because it forces the singers to listen to themselves instead of listening to, and ultimately depending on, the sound of a piano or another instrument. Even a teacher's voice can become a crutch for students. As you teach, occasionally stop singing and just listen. This is especially important during rounds. When it comes time for students to perform, you may add whatever instruments you have available. Some teachers let the students sing along with a tape recording. I am not in favor of this for many reasons. It doesn't help their intonation. It is impossible to take ownership of the music and make your own changes when you have the unchanging taped background. My main objection, however, is that singing is a firsthand experience and taped music is secondhand. I believe that all music making should be a firsthand musical experience.

If you have some students with little or no confidence, students who would rather die than be singled out to sing a note in front of others, do not worry. With the entire class, do a lot of fun call and response clapping, talking, and singing. Start with the least threatening activity, clapping. You clap a rhythm, they echo. Keep the beat going as you change the patterns. Keep it simple. Then progress to call and response speaking. For example: "My name is Jennifer—My name is Jennifer. This is a Monday—This is a Monday," and so on. Then sing simple call and response phrases such as,

"The sun is shining—The sun is shining. But the clouds are gray—But the clouds are gray," and so on. Use only two notes. Which two notes? Use the sol and mi descending thirds I mentioned before—the "na na" notes. By doing lots of nonthreatening call and response work, you are helping both to build students' confidence and teach in-tune singing.

In conclusion, the techniques for in-tune singing are:

1. Create a supportive environment.
2. Sing the "oo" sound in a comfortable range.
3. Using inner hearing, have the students hear the note in their heads.
4. Once the students hear the note, have them repeat it.
5. If it doesn't work, try again, perhaps with a lower pitch.
6. Go through the same steps with different pitches.
7. Have children hear and repeat the pitches sol and mi. Gradually add more notes.
8. Constantly check on the progress of each student, with lots of support.
9. Gradually sing more difficult songs, including rounds.
10. Encourage children to use their higher voices. Sing softly.
11. Sing a cappella (without instruments).

Theoretically, it is possible that you will never have to use the above steps if you teach only songs that are within the children's vocal ranges. Chapter 12 talks about appropriate ranges by age groups and about how to find the best songs.

We have become very accustomed to the false notion that children and adults who sing out of tune will always sing out of tune. It may seem preposterous to say that all hearing people can sing in tune or that anyone can teach them to sing in tune. These things are not preposterous. My advice on in-tune singing is based on twenty years of experience.

Try these techniques. You need to be confident that they will work. You will need to be patient. You will need to be supportive. You will want to smile. And when your class of smiling children sings with that miraculous ringing quality that comes with great intonation, you will want to dance on your desktop because you will see and agree that it was worth working on. You will have reached that transcendent leap from feeling confidence to feeling awe.

Using the Power of a Song's Tradition

· ONE OF the major points of this book is that singing songs can be a very powerful experience. As pointed out in the first part of this book, there are countless examples of how sound and, in particular, singing can affect the body and mind in powerful ways. The first part of the book also discussed the many cultural ways that music affects us. A seemingly ordinary song can become very powerful when we tell its story: who wrote it and why, who sings it and why, what the cultural traditions rooted in the song are that help to give it power. Singing songs can make us more powerful. And singing powerful songs can make us even more powerful.

I mentioned in chapter 5 the student who had learned the South African anthem "N'Kosi Sikeleli Africa" from me. He had later seen Nelson Mandela speak in Boston and had sung along with the anthem at that incredible moment. Singing that powerful song had made him more powerful. All the meaning of the song, the traditions of suffering and hope behind the song— it all came home to him. He felt a sense of unity with the people of South Africa.

If my student had known nothing about the song, all the connections could not have been made. The song's power was not in its melodies or rhythms—the power was in its tradition.

In chapter 6, I explained how to teach the song "Thula Klizeo." Along with teaching the words and notes, I taught the meaning and traditions behind the song. I taught the concept of "stomping quietly" to show resistance to apartheid in a way that will keep you out of jail. The quiet stomp says to the world, "I am powerful and no one can take that power from me."

George Brandon and Ysaye Maria Barnwell, when teaching songs from the African American tradition, always explain the traditions in detail. As I have said before, they go to great lengths to give the singer a real feel for the song. You almost feel as if you were with the originators of the song—you feel their sadness, you understand their expectations.

What Is a Song's Tradition?

The hymn "Amazing Grace" has been a popular song throughout the world, especially since Judy Collins recorded it on her *Whales and Nightingales* album. Bill Moyers did a wonderful hour-long tribute to the song for PBS television. During the tribute, singers ranging from Judy Collins to Jessey Norman sang the great song. Sacred harp singers sang it. Gospel singers sang it. It was shown that the song is embraced by many cultures: by black people, white people, all people—we all own it.

Bill Moyers gave a detailed account of the Englishman who wrote the powerful words to the hymn. His name was John Newton. Early in his life John Newton had made his living in the slave trade, sailing back and forth between West Africa and the Americas selling his fellow human beings for profit. On one of the trips across the Atlantic he was changed by the presence of God in his life. He returned to England where he became an Anglican clergyman and an activist in the antislavery movement. He wrote "Amazing Grace" at the turn of the nineteenth century. When you consider this historical background, the song takes on a whole new and powerful meaning (the hymn is printed in chapter 11).

Here are some questions to ask about each song you lead. Who wrote it? When was it written? Where was it written? In what culture was it written? Does the song have a message?

We can look at a song like "Happy Birthday to You." With a little research you will find that it was written by two sisters who taught kindergarten in England. In 1893 the sisters published a booklet of songs with a song called "Good Morning To You" that later became "Happy Birthday to You." The song's message is obvious. The song is now one of the best known songs in the English-speaking world. The copyright is still legal—a team of international investors recently bought the song for a price in the seven figures. They will get their money back, as every time the song is sung in a movie, television show, or recording, the company receives royalties.

We have answered the above questions concerning "Happy Birthday to You," but something is still missing. We need to ask a few more questions. Ethnomusicologists ask: How is the song sung? How is it taught? Where and when is it sung? Can it only be sung at certain times and in certain places? Is it sacred? Is it secular? Is it healing music? Is it classical music? Is it folk music? Is it from an aural tradition? Is it from a written tradition? How does the song help give identity to the people of the culture who sing the song?

Most of this is obvious in the case of the song "Happy Birthday to You," but let's examine the cultural aspect of the song. It is not a sacred song, but it has ritual elements. For me, blowing out birthday candles would be unthinkable without the song. It is an expected ritual, one that is supposed to repeat every year. It is one of the few acknowledgments of life's changes that we have in our culture. Cultures around the globe constantly celebrate time passages like the changes in the seasons. Life passages like baptisms, puberty rituals, marriage, and funerals are important to acknowledge. There is a huge diversity of rituals to mark these events. When seen from this context, "Happy Birthday to You" takes on a new cultural meaning. Children should also understand that while the song is known throughout the world, most cultures have their own birthday songs and rituals.

Let us ask the same questions about the song "Wearing My Long Winged Feathers" from chapter 7. Here is the text:

> Wearing my long winged feathers as I fly (2x) I circle around,
> I circle around the boundaries of the earth.

I know that the song is Native American, but I do not know from which nation it comes. For all I know it could be a New Age imitation composed in the Native American style. What I do know about the song, however, is quite exciting.

We know a lot about the general culture of Native Americans. There are some commonalties that ring true for many Native American groups. These are ancient traditions. They need to be honored. A Native American colleague of mine told me once, if you sing a fire invocation song, you had better expect fire. If you have no intention on lighting a fire, then you must preface the fire song with an announcement that you honor the song and that you do not wish for there to be a fire here.

Something similar could be said in introducing the song "Wearing My Long Winged Feathers." We will not wear feathers and we will not be dancing "around" the earth, but we honor the tradition behind the song. As another option you could have everyone form a circle and, yes, you could dance "around" the earth.

In introducing this song, the concept of the circle would be an obvious place to start. Many Native Americans believe that all things are part of a circle. All things within the circle are alive and move in cycles. The image of the circle can be seen in artwork and sacred images like prayer wheels and Navaho sand paintings.

There is a sacredness to space. The Navahos call this *hózhóó*, meaning that "the place is beautiful." In chapter 2, I talked of the Native American concept of walking in beauty. To walk in beauty is to walk in harmony with all things. This means that in addition to meaning "the place is beautiful," the word *hózhóó* also means "the place is in harmony." The place is the circle and all things are in harmony within this circle. When singing "Wearing My Long Winged Feathers," the words "I circle around the boundaries of the earth" take on special significance. It says that we are all part of the sacred circle. It says that this space, right here, right now, is special and important. It says that we walk in beauty—in harmony with the earth. I find this to be very powerful.

A song-leading student once asked, "What if I want to teach 'Humpty Dumpty?' It has no tradition, so how can I make it powerful?" My reaction was simple and obvious, "No tradition? What are you saying? The tradition of nursery rhymes is a proud and ancient tradition passed down from generation to generation." Sometimes we need reminding that there was once a time when televisions and video games did not exist, and that communities routinely gathered to sing, dance, and tell stories.

If you are teaching "What Shall I Do with a Drunken Sailor?" you would need to learn something about the tradition of sea chanties or a sailor's life at sea. You might want to explain some of the sailing terms used in the song. You would do everything you could to make the tradition of sailing and work chanties come alive. I have actually had students pretend to be sailors. I ask them to hold an imaginary rope and to pull at a certain time in the lyrics. "To me way hey, to me way-o! We'll pay Paddy Doyle for his [pull] boots!" You repeat the song (it takes a long time to pull up a sail). You add many variations: "We'll all shave under the chin . . . We'll all drink plenty of milk." The action of pulling on the rope, of course, gives the song that little extra meaning. (And it's fun.)

With a song like "What Shall I Do with a Drunken Sailor?" you would also want to know whether the song is from a classical or a folk tradition.

Classical and Folk Music Traditions

There are differing definitions of the terms *classical music* and *folk music*. As with all definitions, there are often exceptions to the rules.

Any composition where the notes are fixed or the same for every performance, never changing, is a classical piece of music. Beethoven's Fifth Symphony can be played faster, slower, louder, or softer, but the notes must remain as he wrote them. Beethoven's Fifth Symphony is a classical piece of music.

Europe is not the only culture with a classical tradition. China, Indonesia, Japan, India, and West Africa all have their own classical traditions, each unique in their own ways, but each unchanging in their composition. A classical drum piece from Ghana, for example, may have been composed long ago by ancestors. Each of the many complicated layers of rhythm must be played exactly as the ancestors created them. Over these rhythmic patterns the master drummer is allowed to improvise, but again, based on a strict set of rules set down from the ancestors.

Folk music exists in all cultures of the world. Like the classical music of

West Africa, it is passed down generation to generation—but unlike the West African music, it does not belong to the ancestors. Folk music belongs to us, the folk. Because it belongs to us, we are allowed to change it, fit it to our needs as new occasions arise. A spiritual becomes a civil rights song with the change of a few words. The hymn "Amazing Grace" becomes a gospel song or a bluegrass song or an art song depending on who is singing it and in what cultural context it is being sung. The song has entered the realm of folk music. It is allowed to change.

Bernice Johnson Reagon, leader of the singing group Sweet Honey in the Rock, was leading a song at a civil rights meeting in the early 1960s. She was singing the African American hymn "Over my Head." The words begin:

> Over my head I see Jesus in the air (3x),
> There must be a God somewhere.

As with many African American hymns, the same words are repeated with key words being replaced, for example, "Over my head, I hear music in the air." In the spirit of the civil rights singing tradition, Bernice Johnson Reagon recalls that she suddenly felt a sense of ownership. She started singing "Over my head, there is freedom in the air." In that moment, she experienced what I feel is important for all song leaders to understand, that folk music, when owned by the singer, becomes truly powerful.

How does folk music evolve? People add or rewrite verses. Melodies change. A drinking song becomes a hymn. A hymn becomes a national anthem or is adapted to become a freedom chant. Cultural styles merge to create something new. Zulu chant and English hymnody merge to create powerful new a cappella music from South Africa. Elements of European hymnody and West African chant forms merge in North America to become the spirituals. Improvisational elements of synagogue music merge with East European dance music to create the great Klezmer musical traditions. New traditions are constantly evolving. I mentioned Paul Simon and Peter Gabriel before, two pop artists who are drawing from the diverse traditions of world music. They are carrying on the folk process of making the music their own—then flying with it.

Woodie Guthrie, who penned "This Land Is Your Land," would constantly adapt old songs, giving them new words or changing their melodies. The song "This Land Is Your Land," although written by Woodie Guthrie, continues to evolve as folk music should. Guthrie's fellow singer, Pete Seeger as well as others, have added new lyrics to the song.

The folk song magazine *Sing Out!* is always full of excellent examples of songs that have changed. They often give the before and after versions.

Too many of us treat all music as if it were classical music. Too often we wouldn't dare change a note or word of a folk song. This is partly because of a new phenomenon in this century—recorded music. When a folk song gets recorded, it becomes fixed. We can play the recording a million times and it will always sound the same. In a way, the folk song, when recorded, becomes classical according to the definitions I have set. I argue that it becomes even more classical as we often want to sing the recorded song only as we have heard it.

If folk music is to survive, it must continue to evolve. We must take ownership of it again. A moment ago I mentioned the tradition behind the chanty "What Shall I Do with a Drunken Sailor?" I said we needed to know one more thing about it—was it from the classical tradition or the folk tradition? Knowing that it is from the folk tradition makes a huge difference in how we teach and sing the song. As will be discussed in chapter 11, we can add new words, change the melody, the rhythm, the harmony, and the texture. As long as we honor the song's tradition, we can make changes— we can make the song our own, thus making it far more powerful.

Recorded music has had another huge influence on all music on the earth. Music has become highly commercialized. The companies that record and sell music do it on a profit basis. They need to make money in order to stay in business. They sell what we want to hear. As I mentioned in chapter

5, people in cultures around the world are drawn to the Western pop music. Their own music borrows heavily from rock and roll and the other pop traditions. West African juju rock has elements of reggae and Hawaiian pedal steel guitar music. Thai rock has a heavy flamenco influence. The extremely popular film music of India mixes traditional Indian elements with a delightfully slick Las Vegas sentimentality. These are all wonderful new forms of music.

Unfortunately, when something is gained, something else is lost. The ancient traditions of music are slowly disappearing. Ethnomusicologists everywhere are currently working to record the musical traditions of the world before these traditions die. The South African composer Joseph Shabalala has founded an organization dedicated to the preservation of the traditional music of South Africa—The Mambazo Academy of South African Music and Culture, 1619 Broadway, Suite #540, New York, NY 10019. Entire governments, such as that of Ghana, have, for years, sponsored cultural research and preservation. I feel that it is essential that these traditions survive somehow. This is another reason why it is so important to honor the traditions behind songs.

How Do You Learn About a Song's Tradition?

Given the importance of knowing a song's tradition or story, how can you find this information? An excellent source is the multiple volume *New Grove's Dictionary of Music and Musicians*, which examines the music of literally thousands of cultures. Each segment contains an excellent bibliography, (albeit twelve or more years old). More and more how-to books are being published that provide practical information on the music of many cultures. Unfortunately, the people who know the most about the music of world cultures, the ethnomusicologists, do not write how-to books, nor does the university system, within which they work, encourage them to do so.

There are publishers that are extremely helpful for teachers looking for music from diverse traditions. These publishers are very good at describing the cultures behind the musical pieces. The Resource Guide at the end of this book contains many important publishers. Each will send catalogs if you request them. I especially recommend World Music Press. Judith Cook Tucker, its publisher, has issued many books with tapes that are extremely teacher-friendly. I also recommend World Music at West, Tara Publications, Ladyslipper Catalog, Singout Corporation, Dove Music, Alfred Publishing, DeKay's House of Music, and The Soar Corporation.

The *Sing Out!* publications often give background information on each song. Accompanying the song "Red River Valley," for example, are the names of the song writers, the date it was written, and information on how the song was sung by settlers on their move West.

When researching the background of a song or a song's tradition, ask the questions I listed earlier in this chapter. Keep a three-ring notebook and/ or computer file containing the songs you learn. As you enter each song, also

enter where you found the song as well as everything you know about the song's background and tradition.

In addition, don't be afraid to ask people from the cultural groups you are studying to come to your classroom and talk with your students. People often feel honored to be asked to do this. Be sure to spend some time talking with them first so you don't go into the session with inaccurate stereotypes. I invited a member of the Crow Nation to speak for a class once. She brought her "heart drum" and explained that the skin on the drum had to be tight for it to sound good—wet weather can cause it to be loose. A student asked what the correct Native American technique for eliminating the moisture in the drum was. We were expecting our guest to say that she lit a sacred fire, then proceeded with a secret ritual. Instead, she answered that she heated the drum-head using an electric hair dryer.

Choose Powerful Songs

At the beginning of this chapter I mentioned my former student who felt connected to the world when he heard or sang the anthem "N'Kosi Sikeleli

Afrika.'' This sense of connection is the result of an understanding of the tradition behind the song.

The earth has always been full of diversity including diversity of cultures. Now, in the twentieth century, this amazing diversity has brought us together. We now can feel connected with music that we never would have known a hundred years ago. A nurse from Seattle may feel a connection to the soothing and healing music of the Akha Pygmies of sub-Saharan Africa. A teacher in Holland may play recordings of Navaho chants to meditate to. A Texas rancher may feel a connection with Celtic music. That Celtic music may become his music—central to his identity as an individual. Every December, millions of people of all faiths from many nations gather in their communities to sing Handel's Messiah. The great masterpiece becomes their music. A Japanese merchant joins a thousand other people to sing ''Hallelujah.'' It becomes her music. Its tradition becomes her tradition.

Powerful singing is our goal. Powerful songs come from powerful traditions. There are many dull songs in the world today—songs with little or no tradition behind them—songs with little or no power. Dull songs encourage dull singing. Powerful songs create powerful singing.

Given the choice, I always choose powerful songs from diverse cultures—songs that are steeped in tradition. From experience I know that children are charged by this kind of music. It not only appeals to them, but it lights a great fire within them, allowing them to shine with their fullest potential.

Chapter 12 will go into greater detail on how to choose songs, with a section on finding the appropriate songs for different ages.

How to Make Your Songs More Exciting

. . . . PREVIOUSLY I spoke of the evolution of music and the importance of the emotions in that evolution. Singing has always been a way of sharing our emotions whether the songs we sing reflect bluesy sadness or jubilant love. We can choose songs to fit our mood at each moment. As song leaders, however, we can do much more. We can actually alter the moods of others. By leading a slow meditative chant, we can create a calm state of mind. By leading a humorous rousing song, we create a mood of joy. I always like to end my sing-alongs on a high emotional level with a song of great compassion, an antiapartheid chant or civil rights song, for example. The energy used in singing such a song helps to create a compassionate sense of community.

By emphasizing the tradition of a piece, such as the tradition of an antiapartheid chant, you help to bring out strong emotions in singers. Emotional reactions, however, can also be brought out by the nature of the music itself. In many cultures, for example, a song in a major key with an upbeat melody like "Twinkle, Twinkle Little Star" will create a happy mood.

Rhythmic entrainment is the habit of living systems to synchronize with others' rhythms or pulses, whether these rhythms are people breathing in unison, soldiers marching to the same beat, or children responding to the rhythm of drums by moving to the pulse. Singers of all ages will usually entrain with the pulse of the music, which results in simple changes of mood.

Choosing the Song

When we are leading songs, it is essential to know that the music we choose will affect people in some way. It is also important to know that many folk songs can be changed in some way to create whatever affect we wish.

With folk music, you own the song. It is your song to adapt and change as you wish, as long as you respect the tradition from which the song comes. This process of adapting music is called *arranging*. Many people think you need a doctorate in music in order to understand this process. Arranging a song, however, can be as simple as singing the song higher or lower or speeding it up or slowing it down. Any of those changes will affect the mood of the song, as you will see in a moment.

One simple question that arrangers ask is, "What effect do I want this song to have on the singers?" For example, do I want them to cry in their seats afterward or to jump up and down with joy? If I am leading songs for young children just before rest time, I would want to end the song in a calm manner. If the children have an energetic activity coming up, I might give the song a rousing ending.

Singing with power means expecting miracles at all times. If you can make a song more powerful by making some small changes, do it! Take ownership of the song and breathe fire into it. Expect miracles!

Let's begin by discussing the beautiful song "Cumbayah"—a song that can produce tears, cheers, or yawns, depending on how it is done.

Cumbayah   Trad. African American

You begin by remembering the song's tradition and meaning. As with many old songs within the folk tradition, no one can be exactly sure about a song's origins. Some believe that "Cumbayah" came from Western Africa to North America as early as the nineteenth century. Others believe that the song had African American origins and somehow became known in West Africa and then returned again to North America. The words "come by here" are often given as the translation. The song is traditionally sung slowly, in harmony, a cappella.

Re-creating the Song

The group Sweet Honey in the Rock recorded a wonderful version of this song on their *All For Freedom* album. Their changes were simple, but extremely refreshing. They sped the song up, giving it more energy. They jazzed up the rhythm, giving it a calypso feel. They added a gospel-style ending. There is a traditional option in gospel music of repeating the last phrase or another appropriate phrase at the end of a piece. Sweet Honey In The Rock ended each verse by repeating the last phrase, "Oh Lord, a-Cumbayah. Oh Lord, a-Cumbayah. Oh Lord, a-Cumbayah, a Cumbayah."

Add harmony and some simple percussion instruments, and you have a very powerful song, certainly very different from the original slow version. At the end of the song, you can repeat "Oh Lord a-Cumbayah" many times with someone singing a gospel-style improvisation over the rest of the singers.

Before providing greater detail on the many changes one can make to a song, let me explain three simple gospel vocal improvisation techniques as taught by gospel expert Horace Boyer. The most common is one in which a soloist plays with the existing words of a song, repeating them with different melodic and rhythmic variations. So in the song "Cumbayah," the soloist could improvise on the words "Come by here" or "Someone's prayin' Lord" or simply "Oh, Lord." A second improvisational technique is to use the words and sometimes the melody from another song. One could, for example, sing the words to the spiritual "This Little Light Of Mine" over the repeated refrain of "Oh Lord a-Cumbayah." A third kind of improvisation is one in which the soloist tells a story or preaches a message. The song "Cumbayah" could inspire, for example, a story about life's journeys. One could then tell a biblical journey story or preach about one's own journey. The possibilities are limitless.

It is important to remember that all three improvisational styles should be sung with respect for the gospel tradition. The singing should never become a lampoon.

The rest of this chapter will discuss simple ways to change songs to alter their moods or to make them easier or more exciting to learn. Use your imagination. As you read, think of the songs you are fond of and the changes you could make. By using your creativity as a song leader, you can make any song an exciting and meaningful experience.

As I have said, always begin with the tradition of the song itself. If, for example, the song is a spiritual, then let the power behind the spiritual tradition be your guide—the spiritual is a freedom song, full of compassion, born of pain, anger, and hope. You can make all the changes in the world, but unless your singers feel the power of the song's tradition, the song will not be sung at its fullest potential. Your changes should not dishonor the traditions.

Because I use the song "Amazing Grace" often as an example of a song to change, it is provided here for reference.

Amazing Grace   by John Newton

Amazing Grace
by John Newton (1725–1807)

1. Amazing Grace! How sweet the sound
   That saved a wretch like me
   I once was lost but now I'm found
   'Twas blind but now I see.

2. 'Twas grace that taught my heart to fear
   And grace my fears relieved
   How precious did that grace appear
   The hour I first believed.

3. The Lord has promised good to me
   His word my hope secures
   He will my shield and portion be
   As long as life endures.

4. Thru many dangers, toils and snares
   I have already come.
   'Tis grace that brought me safe thus far
   And grace will lead me home.

5. When we've been here ten thousand years
   Bright shining as the sun,
   We've no less days to sing God's praise
   Than when we first begun.

1. *Changing the form:* The form of a song is the order of its sections. The original form of "Cumbayah," for example, has the phrase "Cumbayah, my Lord, Cumbayah" sung three times followed by the phrase "Oh Lord, Cumbayah." By repeating the last phrase, the group Sweet Honey in the Rock changed the song's form. This gospel ending can be used for many songs. Try repeating the last phrase of "This Little Light of Mine," "Let it shine, Let it shine, Let it shine," or the last line of "Amazing Grace," "Twas blind, but now I see."

Songs with choruses that repeat after each verse comprise a prominent folk song form. Woody Guthrie's classic "This Land Is Your Land" is a great American classic. When teaching it to younger children, however, you can make a simple adaptation. Teach the younger children the chorus only and have the verses sung by you or by older children.

You may decide to sing only a single verse of a song over and over, particularly if it is a slow song. You can then make other changes as you go along. For example, most people know only one verse of "Amazing Grace." You can repeat that verse many times with simple variations.

2. *Changing the words:* Ruth Crawford Seeger, in the introduction to her classic collection *American Folk Songs for Children* (see Bibliography), said that folk songs "are always ready to grow. They are forever changing, adapting themselves to meet new situations and needs" (p. 23). She continues by giving a humorous example: "A frog goes courting with a six-shooter instead of sword and pistol."

Both the American Union movement and the Civil Rights movement of this century were well known for adapting old songs for new purposes. The phrase "Woke up this mornin' with my mind and it was stayed on Jesus" became "Woke up this mornin' with my mind and it was stayed on Justice."

The tradition of changing words is still very much alive today, and you are allowed to make changes just as long as you do it with respect.

Political sensitivity has become an important issue in our schools and cultural institutions. Within a multicultural framework, all people must receive the respect they deserve. For song leaders, this often means changing words that are sexist, ageist, racist, or that show disrespect toward people with disabilities. One must be careful, however, not to be overzealous in criticizing traditional words. I was once chastised for singing the song "This Little Light of Mine." I was told it was racist. In that the song is an African American spiritual, I was quite surprised by the criticism. I was told, however, that the song referred to the light as being good; therefore, anything that was dark was bad. Issues of white and black, light and dark, should be taken seriously as there are many songs that are racist in the use of these words. However, the concept of light as a spiritual source is so universal that no one need be offended by its use in a song.

People sensitive to the issue of gender classification in songs often suggest changing words like "mankind" to "humanity" and the gender of the word "Lord" from male to female or to neither. I have no trouble with these changes just as long as they respect the traditions of the songs. If, for example, one is singing an African American spiritual that says, "My Lord, He troubled the water," it would be an insult to the spiritual tradition to change the gender of the words. For the people who wrote the spirituals in the days of slavery, the image of God was very clear and therefore vital to the nature of the song. It would be like changing the words to Handel's *Messiah*. Admittedly, the words to spirituals were changed to create civil rights songs, but the spirit of freedom and defiance present in the original spirituals remained intact. The changes were made from within the tradition.

The subject of changing words in songs can be controversial and, like the subject of celebrations (to be discussed in chapter 13,) there is always a need for dialogue by teachers, parents, and students. I try very hard to avoid all controversies, but I find that no matter how hard I try, I often end up upsetting somebody. This is the nature of our world. Cultures clash sometimes. I see this conflict as a necessary part of our evolution.

A fun and harmless way of changing words is to simply play with them. Sit down with children and improvise—make up new words on the spot. As Ruth Crawford Seeger says, "Let improvisation on the words be as spontaneous as possible. Let it grow out of the moment, the day, the child, and you" (p. 27). Children and adults love this activity. The old children's song "Heads, Shoulders, Knees, and Toes" can become "Flies, Mosquitoes, Worms, and Bugs." If a class is studying the weather, they can change the words to "Clouds, Raindrops, Fog, and Mist." Have fun with changing words.

3. *Changing the speed or rhythm:* Changing the speed of a song can bring about an immediate change in mood. Sing the first verse of "Amazing Grace" a few times at a medium tempo, then sing it fast with a gospel feel, clapping on the offbeats (beats two and four in a four-beat pattern). Now sing it very, very slowly, holding each syllable for a long time. You can feel the changes; they are refreshing, to say the least. Try these simple changes with "Swing Low, Sweet Chariot."

Changing the rhythm of a song can mean something very simple, such as giving the song a rock or reggae beat. It can also mean syncopating the rhythm, which basically means "jazzing it up." Sing "She'll Be Comin' 'Round the Mountain" with a very straight, unjazzy rhythm. This is the way the song appears in most publications. Now swing it, which is to say, sing it with a jazzy rhythm. (Technically, this means that you subdivide each beat into three rather than two.)

If a song is traditionally sung with three beats in each measure, it is sometimes possible to add or take out beats in the measure. The hymn "Amazing Grace," for example, can be sung with four beats in the measure:

A / maz - - ing / Grace - - how / sweet - - the / sound
  1 2 3 4 / 1   2   3   4 / 1   2   3   4 / 1

Or it can be sung in a fast eight:

A / maz - - - - ing / Grace - - - - how / sweet - - - - the / sound
  1 2 3 4 5 6 7 8 / 1 2 3 4 5 6 7 8 / 1 2 3 4 5 6 7 8 / 1

4. *Changing the range:* Like the speed of a song, the range is very important in setting the mood. Obviously, it is best to sing songs in the range most comfortable for everyone involved. Singing a song in a higher range, however, can give the song a shimmering quality, particularly if it is sung in tune. Singing a song lower can give it a special richness. Experiment with a variety of songs. You may be surprised with the results.

5. *Changing the melody:* Many melodies are intended for solo singing as opposed to group singing. To adapt such songs, it is sometimes necessary to simplify them, particularly the rhythm. With pop songs, everyone will want to sing the melodies the way they have heard them, but we remember the little details differently. One student imitating Aretha Franklin or Sting can be fun, but thirty could be pure chaos. Sometimes the teacher simply has to say, "Everyone do it my way." You then sing a simplified version of the melody. This may bother some students because they want to sing familiar songs exactly as they hear them. You must insist that you are making the song into *our* song—we cannot do that without singing it our own way.

You can add blues notes to a melody if the style warrants it. There are eight notes in a major scale. Blues notes work best on the third, fifth, and seventh notes of the scale. Simply bend the notes by singing them slightly lower. The same notes are bent in singing country music, except with a bit of a twang added on.

Most melodies in the European American and African American styles are either in the major or minor keys. The song "Three Blind Mice" is in a major key. The songs "Wade in the Water," and "Shalom Chaverim" are in minor keys. You can radically change the mood of a song by changing its mode from minor to major or vice versa. Sing "Twinkle Twinkle" slowly in a minor mode. The normally delightful song becomes mysterious and haunting (and it's still delightful).

6. *Changing the harmony:* Too many of us are afraid of the word *harmony*. The word conjures up impossibilities—great, unreachable walls that are accessible only to the talented. Let's tear down these walls, shall we? Most harmony consists of three notes sung simultaneously. These three notes are called "triads." I will call them chords, although the term *chord* can apply to harmonies with many notes in them. The triad chord consists of a low note, a middle note two notes above, and a top note two notes above that. The range or voicing of these three notes can be altered with the bottom note sung high or the middle or top note sung low. The triad remains the same. In other words, a triad made of the notes F, A, and C can also be voiced A, C, and F or C, F, and A. All that this means is that for any given note, you can harmonize above it or below it and the triad or harmony will remain the same.

F,A,C   A,C,F   C,F,A

When teaching how to harmonize, I ask people to find a note that sounds good and keep singing that note until it doesn't sound good any more—then find a new note.

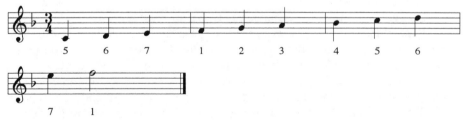

5   6   7   1   2   3   4   5   6

7   1

This means that the old chord has been replaced with a new chord. How do you find your new note that is in harmony with this new chord? Let's do some simple math. Again, there are eight notes in the scale, with the first and last note being the same. A scale could be sung using the numbers 1, 2, 3, 4, 5, 6, 7, and 1 (or 8). Let's say that your first chord used notes 1, 3, and 5. Your second chord used notes 4, 6, and 1 (1 and 8 are the same). This means that if you were singing 5 in a chord using 1, 3, and 5, you can either go up one note to 6 or down one note to 4, both of which are part of the second chord of 4, 6, and 8.

1,3,5   4,6,1

If your original note was 3, then you can go up one note to 4 or down two notes to 1. If your original note was 1, then you can stay there, because the note is common to both chords.

1,3,5   1,4,6

In other words, your new harmony note will either be two notes away, one note away, or the same note. This is true with all basic harmonies. Try this technique with a simple song like "Amazing Grace." Try different harmonies each time. You don't need to know the names or numbers of the notes. All you have to do is be able to listen to yourself and the group at the same time.

Harmony is a building block in the universe. There is a self-organizing process that happens when we sing in harmony. The same self-organizing principle that shapes a solar system or an atom shapes the harmony of a group. You don't have to be any more aware of what you are doing than a star or neutron is. You simply have to give yourself fully to the process, and amazing things will happen. The universe takes over. If you have ever seen great jazz musicians improvising together, you have witnessed these mighty and mysterious powers at work. Become part of the brave interdependence that is called harmony.

Briefly, here are some other kinds of harmonies:

Parallel Harmony: A harmony that duplicates the melody, commonly a 6th or 3rd above or below the melody. A parallel harmony a 5th or 4th higher or lower will sound like Gregorian Chant (Organum).

Contrasting Harmony: A harmony that has the opposite shape of the melody, usually the bass or low part. For example, if the melody got higher and higher, the bass harmony would go down. This is common in European American harmony but not in African nor African American harmony.

Suspended Harmony: By raising the first or third note of a triad, you create a suspended harmony. It's a warm and fuzzy sound. It usually gets resolved back to the original triad.

Drone: By having one group sing one note only, you create what is called a drone. A drone harmony can give an earthy or mysterious quality to a song. Try singing "Amazing Grace" again with one group holding the second note of the melody (A-*maz*-ing) on a drone.

A Cappella Instrumental Imitation: Singers like Bobby McFerrin and groups like The Bobs have revolutionized a cappella singing. They imitate instruments with their voices and bodies. The sound of bass drum and cymbal, for example, can be chanted as "dvvv-tsss-dvvv-tsss." An electric bass part can be added, then a trumpet or guitar. Use only a few instruments at a time, in addition to the melody. Keep the parts simple and repetitive. Children love this. You can have a cappella drum machines to accompany a rap or hip-hop song.

Whenever a song can be sung with harmony, it should be sung with harmony. Every group of singers should sound as fantastic as heavenly possible. Songs like "There Is More Love Somewhere" and "Thula Klizeo" are easy to harmonize. Ask your singers to make up their own harmonies. For other songs, you may wish to prepare simple harmonies beforehand. You may want to use a portable tape player to help yourself prepare the harmonies. Record the melody and then experiment with harmonies until you find some you like.

Before children begin singing harmonies, it is important that they develop an ear for singing rounds. When they begin to hear the harmonies and are comfortable with them, then they should advance to singing other songs in harmony. As with singing rounds, it is important that the teacher's voice, or an instrument such as a piano, not become a crutch for the students. As with rounds, try to sing harmonies a cappella and occasionally stop singing along with your students. Allow them to fly on their own.

The subject of harmony can get very complicated, particularly when you deal with bass, tenor, cambiata (changing boy's voice), alto, and soprano parts, or with such elements as voice leading, chord progressions, and passing tones. The important thing to remember, however, is that harmony is a natural phenomenon, not an insurmountable wall. When we sing in harmony we sing with a richness that is whole and complete. We sing with power.

7. *Changing the texture*: The word *texture* refers to the combined effect of all the voices and/or instruments, not unlike the texture of materials like wool or rope. Each texture is determined by the materials and how they are put together. In music, imagine the textural differences between a solo violinist and an orchestra.

I'm going to use four big words, but don't let them upset you: monophonic, homophonic, polyphonic, and heterophonic. These are the four principal textures in all the music that is sung in groups on this planet. The simplest texture is monophonic. Quite simply, a monophonic texture is one in which everyone sings the same melody at the same time. Sing "Amazing

Grace'' in unison. Everyone should sound more or less like everyone else. You will be singing with the monophonic texture.

In the second texture, homophonic, groups sing harmony at the same time as the melody is being sung. Again, have a group sing "Amazing Grace," this time in rich three-part harmony. You will be amazed at how natural this is and at how good it will sound. Remember, no instruments!

The third texture is called polyphonic, with groups singing the same melody or similar melodies at different times, as in a round, a canon, or a fugue. When we sing "Row, Row Row Your Boat" as a round, we are singing in a polyphonic texture. Try singing "Amazing Grace" as a two-part round with the second group beginning when the first group gets to "That saved a wretch like me." The words "That saved a " and "Amazing" should be sung at the same time.

There are many songs that can be turned into rounds or sung with a polyphonic texture. You can also sing two or more different songs at the same time (see #9 below).

The final texture is one that most music books ignore, and yet it is the most common choral texture on earth. It is called the heterophonic texture. It is a semi-improvisational texture in which everyone sings the same melody differently, at the same time. With the song "Amazing Grace," one person sings "Ama-zing Grace," holding the second syllable and adding a blues note on the third note. Another person sings the same phrase but goes right to the word "Grace" adding many ornamental notes. A third person interprets the melody in a completely different way. The result creates the rich choral tapestry called heterophonic texture.

Listen to recordings by the group Sweet Honey in the Rock. Their interpretation of spirituals, using the heterophonic texture, will convince you that their style is an exciting and authentic alternative to the European style of singing spirituals with homophonic hymnlike harmonies. Listen to the new Celtic music coming out of Ireland. There is often no harmony nor bass part. The violin, flute, and uillean pipes (Irish bagpipes) are often playing the same melody using the heterophonic texture, each playing the melody differently at the same time. How many of us have listened to Native Americans chant and incorrectly wondered why they couldn't learn to sing their melodies in unison? Quite often, each singer is chanting the melody in his or her own way. We need to understand that the heterophonic texture is an ancient and powerful choral texture. It is a unison made out of diverse parts. It is a marvelous fusion of independent and interdependent forces, much like the universe itself.

Experiment with these four textures. They aren't as complicated as they sound. They can add great variety and power to your group singing.

8. *Changing the style:* There are countless styles of music in every culture on earth. Here are a few styles present in North America: reggae, hard rock, rap, easy listening, the blues, country and western, punk, swing jazz, new age, broadway, Seventeenth-Century Baroque, black or white gospel, cajun, punk country, hip-hop, 12-tone, bossa nova, and fusion. The next time you have to sing a happy birthday song to someone, try it as a jazz song or as a country western torch song. The results can be hilarious or, at the very least, refreshing.

9. *Combining songs:* When you begin to experiment with songs, you begin to see that two or more songs can be sung at the same time with wonderful results. Try singing "Shalom Chaverim" and "Wade in the Water" at the same time. The result is a marvelous cross-cultural blend of songs. You don't need to tell people ahead of time that you are going to do this. The surprise of suddenly singing two or more songs simultaneously can be half the fun of it.

Another example: Sing the refrain of "Star of wonder" from the song "We Three Kings,"at the same time as "Twinkle Twinkle Little Star." The rhythm to "Twinkle Twinkle" would have to be changed slightly to duplicate the rhythm of "Star of wonder." Sing the "Star of wonder" section as a round. Add a drone. Have fun. Play around with the music. Be creative.

The practice of singing two or more songs simultaneously is called partner songs. Like rounds, partner songs are essential for students learning to sing in harmony (see Perinchief, *Honor Your Partner Songs*).

10. *Adding instruments:* The simplest instruments to add to any song arrangement are percussion instruments such as drums, shakers, sticks, and bells. As a general rule, keep them simple and quiet. Children and adults can play on the beat if you give them a little coaching. Usually, people will entrain with the rhythm eventually without much coaching. Don't be satisfied with chaos. As with singing, you have to insist that people do it right. They will, if you want them to.

Many instruments, like the Crow Heart Drum, have spiritual elements. The spirits of the elk or deer that the drum is made of are present in the drum. When the animal was killed, a prayer was made in which the animal was honored. When you play a Crow Heart Drum, the living spirit of the animal enters the player. Talking about this with children greatly increases the meaning and power of the experience.

If there is a piano or Orff-style mallet instrument available, I will often do a simple chant like "Wearing My Long Winged Feathers" (chapter 7) and add a piano or Orff instrument drone on one note. With the piano, I ask whether there is someone in the room who has never played the piano before. I then ask that person to play one or two simple notes over and over while pressing the sustain pedal with his or her right foot (the floor pedal on the right). I then lead the song using the simple drone as an accompaniment. The results can be very lovely. Make sure that the song is simple enough for a single drone, otherwise the results could sound a little off.

Music specialists trained in the Orff technique routinely divide their classes in half. One group sings the song while the other plays mallet and other percussion instruments. It is a wonderful hands-on approach to learning music. It does, however, require training on the teacher's part.

11. *Incorporating movement and dance:* Since most people on this beautiful planet move when they sing, by all means add hand signs, body gestures, or dances to every possible song. Students can dance in place, as with the song "Thula Klizeo," or they can do simple circle dances—there are hundreds to choose from. (See *Dances of Universal Peace* in the Resource Guide.) Remember that multisensory experiences are more powerful than monosensory experiences. Hold hands! Dance! Look at each other! Listen! Sing! Smile! Let go! Take ownership of your songs. Don't be afraid to make the simple changes discussed in this chapter. Have fun.

How to Find Powerful Songs

. . . . PERHAPS THE most challenging aspect of song leading is choosing the right songs and chants. You must choose music appropriate for each age from recordings, books, and word-of-mouth sources that include everything from the generic to the inspirational.

In preparing to choose music, I go back to my four song-leading rules. I look for music that will make the group I'm working with sound excellent. It is sometimes too easy to pick songs that the students already love, like current Top 40 songs. Ultimately the task of sounding like their favorite singers will be frustrating. They won't always sound excellent. If I try to pick only music that they will like, I will suffer a nervous breakdown. It is much easier to teach a group to like the piece you picked than to choose a piece that they will like. And how do you teach a group to like what you pick? You go back to rule one; you make them sound good singing that song. Even with the most picky preadolescent boys, if they know they are doing a song well, they will generally enjoy singing it. This does not preclude singing popular songs. And yes, students can choose their own songs from time to time. You also embrace the cultures and stories behind the songs—make the songs come alive.

Powerful Songs

I prefer to lead powerful songs. What is a powerful song? It is a song that comes from a powerful tradition as well as one that rings with compassion.

It is a song that has charging rhythms that excite the body and transport the mind. It is a song whose meaning fills you with wonder or rage or laughter. It is a song that makes you fully alive when you sing it—that charges your emotions, whether those emotions be hate or love or caring or daring. And what are the clear-cut rules for knowing which songs have power? There aren't any. Because we are all different, a song that excites me may not excite you.

In the folk music process, great songs tend to survive, while mediocre ones disappear over time. You can't lose, therefore, if you pick a tried-and-true folk song from any of the world's folk song traditions. This applies to chants as well. There is another advantage with the older songs. They tend to be steeped in tradition, whether that tradition be the sea chanty tradition or the labor movement tradition. And when the tradition of a song is understood and felt on an emotional level, the song's power increases tremendously.

There are a wealth of "old" styles to choose from: urban blues, country blues, bluegrass, black gospel, white gospel, Broadway musicals, Stephen Foster songs (take out any racist references), Hebrew rounds, Hebrew folk songs, Shaker melodies, sacred harp songs, spirituals, war songs, peace songs, patriotic songs, union songs, civil rights songs, women's rights songs, gay and lesbian rights songs, antiapartheid songs, Native American chants, West African chants, South African chants, Hindu chants, Latin chants, Chinese folk songs, Indonesian lullabies ("Suliram"), country and western songs, rhythm and blues songs, fifties rock and roll, doo-wop songs, sixties rock and roll, cowboy songs, hymns, pattie cake chants, reggae songs, calypso songs, animal songs, Cajun or zydeco songs, Hispanic songs, Chicano songs, French Canadian songs, Hawaiian songs, marching songs, jumping songs, crawling songs, and my favorite, flying songs.

Most contemporary folk and pop songs have not been tested by time. You must use your judgment in choosing which new songs will sound great. Remember that there have been thousands of folk songs from the past that have not passed the test of time—no one sings these songs anymore. Ask yourself, of today's pop songs, which songs will people still be singing a hundred years from now? These will be your powerful songs.

The Strengths of Each Age

Since the principle question is, "What songs will make my group sound good?" we should start by understanding the vocal strengths and weaknesses of each age.

Children aged 3–6 sound best when they are singing, moving, and having a good time. (Come to think of it, this is true of all ages.) The best pitch range is from middle C to G or A. Some children that age can sing incredible ranges, but please remember that many others can't, and if you choose music for those with large ranges, the rest of the children will have to struggle. You will, in fact, be teaching them to sing out of tune since they won't be able to match the pitches.

Children aged 3–6 sound best when they are singing songs with simple words. If there is a lot of repetition in the words, that is even better. The melodies need to be simple with no difficult interval jumps. Again, repetitious melodies will sound better. Melodies with lots of sol-mi intervals are great. When children taunt each other in the playground, their "nana nana" melody is the descending minor third interval of sol to mi.

Children this age tend to live in small worlds with themselves in the center. Therefore, songs that involve them in some way work great. These can be called egocentric songs. Songs about life outside of their worlds don't always work well. Songs in their native language will work the best, but very simple songs like "Thula Klizeo," which use only a few foreign words, will also sound great.

Hand motions and movements should be kept simple, but they definitely should be used as much as possible. Children this age do most of their learning through movement. Use lots of party game songs and songs that use circle or line dancing. Remember to sing a cappella and to let the children sing by themselves as often as possible. By age 5 or 6, they can be singing simple rounds. Also remember that one of the reasons singing is so good for children of this age is that it strengthens the listening process and that, in turn, strengthens all other learning systems.

You may hear a recording of a song or see a printed copy of a song that you feel is perfect for singing with 4- to 6-year olds. The range of the song is perfect, only five notes; but on the recording or printed music, these five notes are much too low. What do you do? Simply sing the song in the range that the students will sound good in. You don't need to be able to play piano to find middle C. A simple pitch pipe is all you need. Once you have learned the melody you want to teach, adjust the range so that its lowest note is around middle C and its highest note is around G. This sounds obvious, but it is a rather common mistake made by song leaders. Don't lead songs in a range that is too low for your singers.

With *children aged 7 to 10* the range of the singing increases. They will sound best if you choose songs ranging from A below middle C up to D! Use the higher range more than the lower. It is better for intonation. Repetitious melodies will still sound fine (they always do), but more complicated melodies will also begin to sound good. Do as many rounds as possible. Do partner songs (two or more songs sung simultaneously). Gradually introduce songs with simple harmonies. The children will most likely have to be taught the harmonies as opposed to your asking them to make up their own. Children at this age need to work at singing in tune. It is a good age to improve intonation.

The subject matter of the songs can begin to expand beyond the children's own horizons. The vocabulary can be more challenging. More songs in foreign languages can be sung. Quite often, these will be the most appealing to the students. Continue to use movement and dance. Perform your songs for others as often as possible. Students should begin to feel comfortable in performance situations. It builds confidence. Besides, performances are celebrations. We need to celebrate as often as we can.

Students aged 11 to 15 are at an age where their emotional world is exploding. My first criterion for young people this age is to choose songs that are tremendously emotional and culturally powerful. Please don't make the common mistake of assuming boys this age hate to sing. If you make this assumption, you may end up picking songs that you know will appeal only to girls, and soon only a few boys will be singing. Boys have amazing voices: magical in my opinion.

The range for voices in the 11 to 15 age group is a few notes higher and lower than for ages 7 to 10. Voices change during the 11 to 15 age group. Girls voices become richer. Boys voices drop an octave. This change in voice can be very gradual, with the strong bass sound developing later in adulthood. For most boys, this jump is extremely awkward, and for a while, they no longer sound great (unless you pick the right music). They can easily loose interest and stop singing. Many adult men stop singing when their voices change.

There are actually three types of male voices at this age. The first is the changed voice. The second is the changing voice, and the third is the un-changed high voice.

The changing male voice has a very small range at first. For most boys with changing voices, their range is from ab to Eb. That is only five notes. The girls will be singing songs with ranges of ten or more notes. If the changing-voice boys are asked to sing along, they will simply have to sing wrong notes, and bad intonation habits will surface. In other words, they won't sound good. As I have said from the beginning, it is essential that everyone sounds great and has self-confidence. The solution is that you will need to choose songs that use simple harmonies. The range these boys are singing in is roughly equivalent to the low tenor range (G below middle C up to D). Many tenor harmonies, will, therefore, sound great.

How do you find songs that have great five-note tenor harmonies? Un-fortunately, this is not an easy task. Some choral publishers publish music that includes selections good for the changing male voice. Look for music that mentions the cambiata. Usually, however, you have to find songs or chants and then add the harmonies yourself. Let us use "Thula Klizeo" as a model. The melody, as shown in chapter 6, goes from middle C to the octave above—too wide a range for the boy with a changing voice. The following is a simple tenor part for "Thula Klizeo." Please note that it uses only three notes. Changing-voice boys will sound great singing this and will therefore enjoy singing it.

The book of South African songs, *Freedom Is Coming* (see Appendix B), has many exciting songs, all with tenor parts perfect for the changing male voice. Many African songs and chants are ideal. The repetition and driving

Thula Klizeo By Joseph Shabalala

Melody: Thu-la Kli-zi - o, Na-la-pa-sey Ki - ya Hey Ki ya,

Tenor Part: Thu-la Kli-zi - o, Na-la-pa-sey Ki - ya Hey Ki - ya,

Na - la - pa - sey Ki - - ya.

Na - la - pa - sey Ki - - ya.

rhythms of the African pieces are, for some reason, attractive to boys this age.

Boys who have sung a lot often have an easier time with their voice changes—sometimes they can sing a range of three octaves, both in the new low voice and their old high voices.

The unchanged male voices will still be singing with the girls. They should be given lots of encouragement because this is an awkward time for them. Some other boys will have fully changed voices and will be able to sing the melody (an octave lower) as well as their own bass parts. The boys with the fully changed voices should sit away from those with the still changing voices so the two groups won't throw each other off. Those with unchanged voices should also be seated apart from the others. If a high-voiced boy is very sensitive to being separated, it would not hurt to place the boy with the tenors—the boys whose voices are just beginning to change. Be sensitive to the needs of the boy with the unchanged voice. Placing him with the girls might not help his self-image much. If this is a big issue, don't separate any of the boys from the girls. Have everyone sit in their usual boy/girl pattern.

With ages 15 on up, choose songs that use lots of harmony. Choose longer, more challenging songs. Have fun. High school and college students can sing with amazing energy and precision. They really can perform miracles, and there is no reason why they shouldn't. The same is true of adults. Unfortunately, many adults, especially men, will have stopped singing in their youth and may have emotional or psychological barriers to singing. When working with these adults, I again choose songs that I know will sound great–always with harmony. These songs and chants are usually short and fairly simple. They are also extremely powerful and rewarding to sing.

At the end of this book are the names and addresses of many music catalogs. You can find song books and recordings of songs from many of the world's cultures and from many song styles. Write and ask for these catalogs. Begin to collect song books and recordings. If you are at a folk festival, check out the books and recordings. The search for great music won't always be easy, but it will always be rewarding. I once heard a concert of Palestinian music on the radio. I recorded it and fell in love with one of the songs called "Bafta Hindi" ["Hindu Cloth"], a humorous song sung by women making fun of men's courtship mannerisms. I was determined to do this song with children. I had to find someone who spoke Arabic to help transcribe and translate the song. My Arab friend was honored that I was doing an Arabic song. I had to teach it to the children who, at first, had trouble with the language and reacted against it. We finally performed it. They sounded great. They felt good singing it. Was it worth the effort on my part? Yes, yes, yes!

When choosing songs from recordings, it is important to listen with imagination. How would this sound sung by my group? What changes will you have to make? With folk music, remember, you own the song; you can change the words, the melody, the speed, the rhythm, the style, the range, and most important, the mood.

Choose easy songs, challenging songs, songs from many cultures, and songs in many styles. Treat each song as sacred. Insist that your group sing it well.

Have fun. Smile.

The Singing Celebration

. . . . ONE FINAL and important aspect of song leading is the all-school singing celebration. Most elementary schools have all-school assemblies three or four times a year. I propose something different: the *weekly all-school singing celebration*—thirty minutes of sing-alongs led by different teachers, students, and guests—a celebration of the school and of all the learning, creativity, and play that energizes the school. I have witnessed how the simple act of singing together affects a school. When I taught K-8 music in Cambridge, the students and teachers met every Thursday morning to sing. It was a tradition that had been part of the school's tradition for a long time. I did not create the tradition, but I certainly fell in love with it. I fervently believe in this practice for all elementary schools.

Celebration

Celebration is many things. It is a unifying experience bringing students, family, and teachers together—creating a community identity. It is important for students to have a sense of identity with their schools. Some schools have created school identity though large art projects like murals to which every classroom contributes a piece of the final masterwork covering whole sections of the school's walls.

Celebration involves the releasing of emotions within a group situation—students laughing together, crying together, creating a sense of awe and wonder—all singing. These emotions, when experienced by everyone in a community, can combine to create great fire, something truly amazing.

Celebration can be a form of profound play—a form of ritual. In such a situation, time and place take on an importance of their own. Time slows down, every moment becomes exhilarating. A combination cafeteria/gymnasium becomes a great concert hall. The ritual of an all-school singing celebration is serious in nature, even though it is joyous—it is controlled play—the creativity of the playground nurtured and allowed to become even more alive.

Celebration involves sharing. I have spoken of how West Africans make music as an act of compassion—an act of generosity. When we make music together, we share with one another. This, alone, is a great reason for embracing singing celebrations—to teach compassion, the act of making the world a more beautiful place through caring for each other.

When the celebration is directed outwardly, toward the world outside of the school, the compassion is magnified tremendously. An example would be an assembly focusing on community efforts like neighborhood cleanup or recycling. Students can celebrate recent world events. When the first free elections were held in South Africa, I attended a school celebration the next day commemorating the event. It was an honor to be there.

I like to think of the singing celebration in the Navaho *hózhóó* way— that the place, the gymnasium or cafeteria, is an important place. Our being here is important. Here there is harmony.

A powerful celebration bonds participants together. I have witnessed how students have become proud of themselves through the simple act of group singing. And just as confidence transcends to wonder, this pride grows into awe. "Wow, I'm great!" Through group singing and celebration, every child gains a strong sense of self-worth. They are performing for each other. It's like having one of your drawings exhibited on the school walls. You are filled with pride—the work of art you created becomes a celebration of you.

"But," some teachers may say, "an assembly like this would be a disciplinary nightmare. The little children will be fidgety and the older students will take it as a joke." These concerns are valid, but if you anticipate these problems, you can eliminate them. I have led hundreds of singing celebrations at many schools. I have always found that good discipline will happen if you insist on respect, and if you expect and demand great results (Rule One: Make everyone sound fantastic). Ultimately the respect that is gained becomes pride and awe; and when the celebration becomes a routine part of their week, it becomes a ritual that all ages will look forward to. A simple disciplinary practice is to wait until there is total silence and attention before beginning the first song.

"But," other teachers may say, "we don't have the time to do weekly celebrations. The teachers are overworked and the students don't have enough time for their studies." I sympathize with both of these problems, but I have seen, over and over, how singing celebrations revitalize an entire school's energy. I have seen students return to their classes eager to resume their studies, taking pride in their work and in their school. I have seen teachers, stressed out by their busy schedules, laughing and playing together in a joyful way through the singing celebration. They too return to the classroom with renewed energy. I have felt the bond that these celebrations create—singing in harmony creates a metaphorical harmony where everyone comes together in a tremendous sense of unity.

I once led a singing celebration where the students and I prepared large props to help magnify the theme of the celebration. We made a giant puppet of St. Brendan, the Irish saint who sailed to Newfoundland in the sixth century. Brendan and his crew became terribly lost. In desperation, they pulled their ship onto a small island that turned out to be a great whale that led them to the new land. The students and I built a wood-framed cardboard whale that was thirty-five feet long. While everyone was singing, this great whale circled the gym/auditorium. A tremendous amount of preparation went into this one celebration. Was it worth it? Absolutely. The time and energy spent in preparing for a celebration is like an investment—an investment in which you get back much more than you put in.

The All-School Celebration

All that is needed for the weekly all-school singing celebration is a large, quiet space such as a gym. Sharing the gym with band practice doesn't work. Students can sit on the floor; a semicircle shape works best, with the youngest children in the front. You can also seat younger students with older students. Discipline improves when the older students assume a position of responsibility rather than a position that invites looking down on the proceedings. For example, at an elementary school where I taught, the middle school students would sometimes go to the kindergarten and first-grade classrooms and escort the younger students to the gymnasium for the singing celebration.

In such a singing celebration, teachers, community members, and students can take turns leading and teaching songs. It is important that the celebration be a community event, not dominated by the music specialist, if your school is lucky enough to have one. Every classroom teacher, after all, has the ability to be a great song leader.

Different classes can learn the songs ahead of time. For example, one class could learn the verses to Woody Guthrie's "This Land Is Your Land." At the celebration, the rest of the school can join in singing the chorus, "This land is your land, This land is my land."

The school chorus could perform, allowing for some songs to be done as sing-alongs with the rest of the school. (I now direct an adult chorus in Boston, The Mystic Chorale. All of our concerts are also sing-alongs.)

A class could write a song, then teach it to the whole school. I believe the act of writing music is a creative act and the creative act is never complete until it is shared with others—until it is celebrated.

Instead of song sheets, overhead projectors can provide words for everyone if needed. The advantage of having the words on the wall is that everyone's heads are up—a better posture for singing. Also, it is easier for you, the teacher, to see who is involved and who is not. As an art project, students can make huge word sheets that can be taped to the walls. This is particularly helpful if you are going to be singing a song that is in a language foreign to the students. I prefer to use many short and simple songs and chants in many languages. Chants tend to be short in duration. When singing them, I find tremendous power in repeating them many times—such repetition can be quite mesmerizing. As you are repeating songs and chants, feel free to make changes, such as doing them faster, slower, higher, lower, or in different styles. Add drums and other percussion instruments. Have students stand. Let them move. Turn the song into a line dance, leading the students around the gym, maybe even the whole school. Examples of chants are "Thula Klizeo" and "Thuma Mina," "Woke Up This Mornin'," "Wearing My Long Winged Feathers," and "There Is More Love Somewhere." Rounds are also forms of chants. When you sing a round, sing it softly with lots of healthy repetition.

The four simple rules set out in chapter 5 should be observed—make everyone sound great, create confidence in every singer, teach the songs as if you were teaching them to yourself, and honor the traditions behind the songs. In addition, the song leader should ask how to make the songs more powerful by taking ownership of the songs and making necessary changes (see chapters 10 and 11).

Finding a Celebration Theme

It is often effective to give the celebration a theme. This is not unlike school assemblies that celebrate everything from Thanksgiving to Flag Day. There are both cultural and religious holidays, including the holidays of many cultural traditions. Celebrations don't have to involve holidays, however. You can celebrate sports by singing songs about football, basketball, or baseball heroes. You can celebrate trains, food, fashion, humor, and history. You could have a celebration of trees and end the celebration by chanting and dancing out to the front of the school to dedicate the planting of a new tree.

Remember that the theme of your celebration may not be as universal as you think it is. For example, many Native Americans consider Thanksgiving a time of mourning. It is the commemoration of the loss of their native land. It also perpetuates the the one-sided view that all early European settlers got along with Native Americans.

Another thing to be careful of is the borrowing of songs or celebrations that should not be borrowed. It is inappropriate to perform Communion at a school or sing songs from a Friday night Sabbath service or from a Navaho Nightway ritual. These are all songs and rituals that belong in their own sacred time and sacred space. As I said before, this should not prevent you from celebrating and singing the songs of these and all other cultures. You simply need to honor the traditions (see chapter 10).

The singing celebration should be for everyone in the school. This borrows from the West African tradition of having no separation between performer and audience performance. This is very different from most all-school assemblies in which classes perform for each other. Because of their long length, these marathon events can often be torturous, or at least unpleasant experiences for the majority involved (or uninvolved). These traditional assemblies are shows, but not always celebrations. When everyone is involved with an all-school celebration, everyone gains a sense of ownership—these are our voices, these are our songs, this is our school.

Celebrations can be integrated with daily curricula. For example, a math class can learn a counting song, then teach that song to the entire school. A social studies class can learn a Hopi chant or an eighteenth-century French round, then share it in a celebration.

Use all kinds of songs and chants. Call and response songs work as great icebreakers in the beginning. Sing rounds, songs with movement, songs that tell stories. Sing both new and familiar songs. Don't be afraid to sing rock, pop, or rap songs. By all means, sing songs in harmony whenever possible. As discussed in chapters 2, 3, and 4, harmony is more than just pretty sounds. Harmony is a metaphor for life itself. Harmony is the way the universe works. By all means, always strive for harmony (this means working toward the goal of having everyone singing in tune; see chapter 9).

Take ownership of the songs. Add drums and percussion instruments. Change the songs. Make a familiar song like "Hey, Ho, Nobody Home" into a rap or a country song.

Involve the students in a schoolwide a cappella rock band. Ask everyone who wants to be a drummer to stand in one area. Have the electric bass players in another section and the lead singers in another place. With a little planning ahead and a little rehearsal in the gymnasium/ concert hall, all kinds of magical and fun things could go on.

Play games with the songs. Do a song where students must stand, then sit in rapid succession. Make it into a competition to see which grades or classes can stand most quietly. I have done a simple game where I ask for student volunteers to analyze the songs. Ever wonder what the round "Row, Row, Row Your Boat" means? You'd be amazed at what a few creative students will come up with. One of my students said that "life was a dream where everyone rows and rows but no one ever gets anywhere."

I held a contest once where we looked for the dumbest song in the world. Students had a week to prepare a song they had heard somewhere. Either as individuals or as a group, they had to teach the song to the whole school. The results were hilarious. I remember that a song about three-day-old pizza was chosen the dumbest song in the world. And I had been rooting for the theme from "Gilligan's Island."

Honoring the Diversity of Traditions

On the serious side, you can invite parents, grandparents, and friends to explain what a song means to them. For example, a grandfather explains how his grandparents crossed the plains in a wagon singing songs like "Red River Valley." He explains what life was like for the travelers. He gives the song a life it wouldn't otherwise have. The presentation ends with everyone singing the song. Find members of your community who were active in the Civil Rights movement. They could talk about a song that moved them, again making the song come alive. I was leading the Yiddish theater song "Donna Donna" once and asked the adults present if anyone had a story to go with the song. The results were very moving. One parent said that her mother had sung the song in a cattle car as she was taken off to a concentration camp in Poland. The woman survived to sing the song with her grandchildren. I cannot sing that song without thinking of her story.

These stories make the music ring with history—the traditions sing to us. We are joined in a powerful way with people of a different time and a different world. We gain a sense of their sadness, their joy.

The music of the celebrations should be drawn from cultures all over the earth. Every celebration should be a minicelebration of humanity—not the unity of humanity, but the diversity of humanity.

In the past twenty years, there has been a movement to remove all controversial subjects from school assemblies. This became a necessity because such celebrations as Christmas had been thought to be universal, but they were not. It came as a shock to many Americans that the holiday of Christmas, when celebrated in school, was offensive to some—even controversial.

I agree that it was time for a change. It is certainly inappropriate to assume that Christmas should be universally worshipped in public schools. By removing all things controversial, however, two things were lost. We lost our diversity and we lost our love for celebration. In seeking a common ground, we tried to pretend that all of us were the same. We are not. We can only find a common ground by accepting and honoring our differences. It is our diversity that makes us strong. And it is through singing and through celebrating this diversity that we identify who we are.

The controversies will still remain. It is up to every school to have a dialogue in order to answer these questions. Can we celebrate our differences? Can we sing songs about different belief systems? Can we sing the occasional sacred song, round, or chant? Can we share in the celebrations of diverse cultures? If we believe in diversity, can we sing Passover songs and Hanukkah songs? Can we celebrate the African American observance of Kwanza? If we believe in honoring diversity, can we sing a Christmas carol? Can we share each other's celebrations and the celebrations of the world?

The United States Supreme Court has made it clear that there must be a separation of church and state. Religions must not be preached in schools. There should be no school-sponsored worship. But celebration is different from worship. And the study of religion is necessary because children need to learn about the diversity of cultures. We cannot understand a culture without understanding something about its religion. We humans use religion as a way of explaining our place in the universe and as a framework for our morality and laws.

Religious events or beliefs can, by their examples, teach important moral lessons. The Passover story, for example, is a powerful story of a people's liberation from bondage. Songs like "Dayenu" carry a powerful message. "Had He only, Had He only brought us out of Egypt, Dayenu (That would have been enough.)" The story of Moses gave hope to the slaves of North America. The story and the songs affect us still. The story bridges across every part of human history and into our future.

When we remove celebrations from cultures, the cultures become dead. They become fossils of their former selves. Make cultures live. Celebrate as the cultures celebrate. Use singing to celebrate life.

Schools that celebrate by singing are energetic schools. Schools where group singing is a weekly event are healthier environments for children. To live without celebration is to live a secondhand life. To celebrate is to be alive at one's fullest.

Troubleshooting

· · · · · · · · · · · · · · · · · · · THINGS DON'T always work out as we hoped. Problems arise. In this chapter are some of the questions I am asked when I lead teacher workshops. Some of these questions may be answered better by your fellow teachers. Don't be afraid to ask for advice. Good teaching cannot take place in a vacuum. We need each other's support and wisdom.

- **What if my students refuse to sing the first time I try?**
  What if they hate singing?

Students who have had little singing experience are often reluctant to sing. Their reluctance, however, should not be seen as antagonism. There are simple steps you can use to familiarize them with singing while breaking down any fears they have of showing their emotions in public, which is part of what the musical experience is all about.

When I am with a reluctant group, let's say a group of junior high school students, I begin with simple call and response activities (see chapter 7)— the less threatening, the better. I like doing rhythms first. I clap simple four-beat rhythms and have them repeat after me. We are capable of doing low, medium, and high claps with our hands. To create the lowest clap, cup both hands as you clap. To create the highest clap, clap the fingers of one hand against the flat palm of the other. Make up rhythmic patterns using low and high claps. As you have students repeat after you, have them join in making up rhythms. Invite them to use some popular rhythms from funk, rap, hip-hop, rock, or country music.

I continue with the call and response activities by having them repeat words or word phrases. This can be as simple as their names or as complex as math equations, poetry, and famous quotes or sayings. Gradually I introduce pitches into the repetitions. Remember, my first rule of song leading is that the group should sound great, so I use simple two-note repetitions (sol, mi) that I know they will sound good doing.

Usually, they are ready to sing something at this point. I teach the first song using lots of call and response. I choose a song that I know they will sound good singing—nothing too difficult at first. Later, I do demanding songs.

Because some of the boys have changing voices, I create simple three-note harmonies for them to sing—harmonies that I know they will sound good singing (see chapter 11).

Students who have never sung before will need to be taught how to sound good. Girls will often sing or try to sing an octave too low. They may be embarrassed to sing in their high beautiful voices, but they must be encouraged to do so. You simply have the class repeat one note—the purpose is for them to discover the power of their voice. With these beginning singers, I tend to use phrases like "the power of your voice" as opposed to "the beauty of your voice." I present the entire singing experience with terms like "strong," "proud," and "mighty." Terms like "beauty" and "elegance" can be a turnoff. Later, when the class is singing like angels, you can use the "beauty" word.

While I am singing with this junior high class, I do simple things to make them sing in tune. I might do some inner-hearing exercises with them where I ask them to hear a note in their heads, then sing it back (see chapter 9). I may have them sing a song with exaggerated nasality as a way to make their normal singing more resonant, or I might use some guided imagery to create the sounds I want (see chapter 8). For example, if I wanted a more energetic sound, I might ask them to imagine striking a drum with every, syllable they sing. If I wanted a smooth sound, I might ask them to imagine that they were floating in the air.

Don't try to go too fast at the beginning. Remember my Rule Two about creating confidence. Students may be reluctant to start. If you expect too much at this point, their lack of confidence may turn into antagonism toward both you and the singing. Remember Rule Three and put yourself in their position. Remember Rule Four and embrace the cultural traditions behind the songs.

But above all, remember Rule One. If they sound good, even on one single solitary note, that will be enough. Let them know they sound good. Let them know they are going to sound better as time goes on. Let them know they are going to amaze themselves and anyone who is fortunate enough to hear them. Don't give up. Even the most antagonistic group can be taught to sing. Start slowly. Break down their fears. Have confidence in the class and in your abilities as a teacher.

- **What if the students aren't afraid of singing, but they find it boring?**

Again, review the rules outlined in chapter 5, especially Rule Four about embracing the cultures behind the songs. If students have a deep awareness of the cultural meaning of a song, the singing becomes a very powerful experience. Combine this with Rule One, making them sound fantastic, and they may find their singing to be far from boring.

Sometimes students build an identity around themselves that is like a wall. For these students, only a certain kind of music is powerful. Everything else is boring. In cases like this, it is often a good idea to start where the student are. Embrace their music, whatever it is. You may not be able to teach a rap, a grunge rock song, or a country ballad, but you can share the music with them. They can play tapes of their music in class. They can perform the songs for each other, assuming the lyrics are acceptable. (Some street music belongs on the streets, not in the schools.)

Never tell students that their music is less powerful than another kind of music. If you denounce their music, you will be guilty of the same crime your students are committing. You will be building a wall around yourself. Learn about their music. Learn about rap, rock, country, hip-hop, reggae, and world music.

When you begin by accepting their music, you can then slowly expand their worlds, breaking down the walls. I have taught the music of J. S. Bach to students who identified with rock and rap. The Bach became just as powerful an experience as their own music. As I said before, young people don't hate Bach, they hate people who like Bach. Take away the perception of stuffiness—show Bach for the amazing genius he was.

What if they still find singing boring? Review chapters 8 through 13. Are you teaching your students how to sound beautiful? Are you teaching them to sing in tune? Are they fully embracing the traditions behind the songs? Are you and they taking ownership of the songs and making appropriate changes in order to make the music more exciting? Are you making the effort to find powerful songs? Are you involving your students in the school's singing celebrations? Answering any one of these questions may help you solve the problem.

- **What if I, the teacher, am terrified of singing, let alone song leading?**

You are not alone in this fear. It is a common anxiety. It is also a problem that can be solved with a little bit of effort.

Chapter 13 spoke of the Singing Celebration, where teachers and students gather on a regular basis to sing. In such an environment, singing becomes very natural. Fears are washed away. Confidence abounds. Everyone is encouraged to lead and share songs. Gradually, as your fear of singing subsides, you will be able to begin leading songs. You may want to start with a small classroom or even with your fellow teachers for a practice session.

At one school where I taught, I began a faculty/parent chorus that met once a week an hour before school. Singing before school had a bonus affect— we felt energized by the singing. It was like a good workout. Another possibility is that you can start a singing support group where you gather with others who share your reluctance to sing. What do you do at these gatherings? You sing. Find some copies of the *Rise Up Singing* songbook. It has thousands of songs in it. There are always enough familiar ones for any group to sing.

Many communities have folk music societies that hold meetings and sing-alongs. Shy singers are always welcome.

Karaoke is a new phenomenon. You can go to a karaoke bar and sing popular songs. The words are projected on a video screen.

Almost every community has a local amateur chorus that welcomes newcomers at certain points in the year. Jump into the fire and join such a group. The evening rehearsals, like the early morning rehearsals, will not further exhaust you—they will revitalize you.

Don't be afraid if a chorus you want to join has auditions. Often, the director simply wants to know if you are confident enough to show up for the audition. My experience as a choral director has been that the confident person can learn to sing well simply because he or she has the right attitude.

And, of course, there's always singing in the shower.

• **What if I have crowd-control problems?**

There are millions of books on every aspect of education, but too few on the subject of discipline. I was an education major in college. I never heard the word *discipline* spoken once. When I began teaching, I had control problems and felt lost and discouraged. I was too proud to ask for advice from my fellow teachers.

My experience since then has taught that there are many forms of discipline. There are highly regimented classrooms where fear motivates good behavior and there are the seemingly anarchistic classrooms where the students good behavior is due to a magical, but hard won, respect for each other. In both cases, it is essential for the teacher to have a deep confidence in her or himself. Students have the ability to know immediately how much confidence a teacher has. As a substitute teacher, I learned the "ten-second rule." If you don't have good discipline in the first ten seconds, you won't get it. Ten seconds is all it takes for the first student to challenge your authority as a teacher. The challenge may be someone bothering a fellow student or an earnest question like, "Can we smoke in class? All the other teachers let us smoke." You must show that authority immediately. By doing so, you set limits.

Discipline can be a problem when you are leading songs. It is very important that you insist on a supportive environment where students are not allowed to laugh at or be condescending to each other. Exciting songs can be too exciting. If you can learn to control the energy of a song, then you will learn how to control a class. If you are leading a series of songs, especially with younger children, have the next song ready when you finish the first. Remember entrainment? If you speak in a fast agitated voice, your students will become fast and agitated.

If you speak in a slow, but energized voice, your students will be calm, yet enthusiastic.

There are many controversies concerning styles of discipline. Every school has its own techniques, some schools offer "alternative classrooms," classrooms with a more creative disciplinary environment. The issue of multi-culturalism is important to discipline, because different cultures have different styles of discipline.

Discuss discipline with fellow teachers. Become acquainted with the different approaches. Without good discipline, no matter what approach you use, your time and hard work as a teacher will be wasted.

- **If I sing out of tune with my students, will they sing out of tune also?**

Probably. If your singing is not focused on the right pitches, the students won't be able to accurately hear what notes they should sing. But this shouldn't stop you from having your students sing.

When I worked as a full-time substitute teacher at a public high school, I taught a different subject every day. I found it was possible to teach subjects I knew little about (like calculus) simply by allowing the students to teach themselves. I was still the teacher, but the students became the problem solvers. For teachers who have not yet learned to sing in tune, the students can help teach the songs.

A volunteer student could learn a song from a tape recording. You could then teach the song using the techniques discussed in this book, except that the student would sing each phrase instead of you. I am not making this up. Many teachers have been using this technique for years.

- **What if I want to teach songs, but I have the voice of an ill-tempered frog?**

Don't ask the students to imitate your voice if you feel your voice sounds like an ill-tempered frog unless you want a classroom that sounds like a diseased swamp. The quality of your voice is not as important as you may think. What is important is that you enjoy singing. The spirit of your singing will effect students far more than your tonal qualities. You can still sing along with them, simply ask them not to model their voices on yours. Besides, your voice does not need to be the one that students imitate. As with the last example, you can use certain voices in the classroom as the models for the sound you want.

Review chapter 8 on how to sing beautifully. There are simple nontechnical ways to improve every voice. And remember not to sing in an intimidating operatic voice. This is a big turnoff for most students.

- **What if I want to use more singing and music in my classroom, but the school administrators or the local school board prevent me from doing so?**

In our need for quick solutions, we often seek the obvious answers. For example, if the students are doing poorly in math and reading, we conclude that they should spend more time studying math and reading. Administrators need to learn that this is not the best solution in the long run. What has to happen is that the students need a healthier and more creative learning environment where the multiple intelligences are emphasized. In such an environment, singing, drawing, and dancing help to charge the body and brain of each student making their academic studies more effective (Gardner 93, 5–34). We do not need to spend more time teaching academic subjects, we simply need to spend our time more effectively.

As teachers, we need to make both parents and administrators aware of the benefits of having music in the classroom—all classrooms. Familiarize yourself with the reasons why music is important. Read the next chapter, "Sixty-Five Reasons Why Singing Should Be Central to Education and to Life." Teach these reasons.

But be careful not to teach these reasons only in the traditional way. If you present your argument to the administrators, request that they sing. Bring a classroom of children to a board meeting and let the students sing or lead a sing-a-long. Allow the administrators to feel at a gut level how powerful singing is. If the administrators sang at their meetings, I guarantee the meetings would be much more efficient and the administrators would be much more likely to support music and the arts at all levels of education. As I have said in this book, sometimes all the words in the world are useless compared to the emotional impact of singing a good song.

- **What if I know absolutely nothing about music? How can I teach music?**

Remember the famous Zimbabwe saying I used at the start of this book? "If you can walk, you can dance. If you can talk, you can sing." Do you remember the next step? "If you sing, you can teach a song."

Also remember, in our Western culture there is a perceived gap between the talented and the untalented. This applies to musicianship, both our ability to understand music and to perform it. But this gap does not actually exist. Yes, there are talented musicians, but the so-called untalented have far more abilities than anyone has previously realized. In most cultures of the world, this gap between the talented and untalented does not exist (Blacking 1984, 43–52).

Your goal is not to prepare your students for concerts at Carnegie Hall. Your goal is to make your students more alive and alert, to bring joy to their lives, and to give them a chance to create powerful identities both as individuals and as communities. We don't need to know anything about music. The music is already within us. We simply need to let it out. We need to allow the light in all of us to shine at its fullest.

Why Is
Music
Necessary?

Sixty-Five Reasons Why Singing Should Be Central to Education and to Life

· Too many school systems view music and the arts as unessential for learning. Music is cut from the budget or given a very low status. The Music Educators National Conference (MENC), the American Choral Directors Association (ACDA), and The American Orff-Schuwerk Association (AOSA) have defended music in our schools for many years. This chapter follows that spirit; it is a defense of music in our schools using both old and new perspectives on music.

Being Fully Human Through Music (This Little Light of Mine)

1. Music is essential to provide cultural identity. Every culture has its own unique music. The music, art, and dance each culture makes and responds to defines that culture. We need music and the arts in order to know who we are.

2. Music is essential for the ongoing evolution of humans. Chanting and singing have played central roles in our evolution thus far. Music was necessary for the evolution of language, which brought us communication; pattern recognition led to memory, and music in ritual gave us self-awareness as well as awareness of the universe around us.

3. One might make the following argument: Rubbing sticks together was once important for humans to be able to make fire, but we now have electric stoves; similarly, singing was once important, but now we have radios. We are no longer in need of firsthand experiences such as making fires or singing. Why make music when we can just as easily turn on a radio or a CD player? Why celebrate, when we can watch a celebration on TV? One might argue that all firsthand experience is an evolutionary dinosaur bound for extinction.

But firsthand experiences like singing are more powerful than second-hand experiences like watching or hearing. It is not enough that there is music everywhere around us—in the movies, on TV, on the radio, on portable tape players, and in the shopping malls. We need to experience music and creative emotional expression firsthand. We need to sing and make music.

4. Children are like stars. Can we tell a star to stop shining? No. Should we tell children to stop shining? No. Yet when music is not celebrated, children don't get the chance to shine like stars.

5. You may remember that self-organization is the tendency of actions to automatically form a balance or harmony. All living things interact in a balanced way, insuring the survival of all life. Many cultures around the planet say that all life is in harmony. Music, because it too is made of harmony, is essential for our lives as it helps to balance or harmonize the brain, the body, and the spirit. Further, it helps to harmonize us with each other—it helps to hold our communities and cultures together.

6. Howard Gardner, who has researched how the brain and the body learn, points out that there are many types of intelligences. One type is musical intelligence. Each form of intelligence helps strengthen the others. Remove one, and the others suffer.

7. Music helps to strengthen the right brain, which is largely responsible for our creative output. We need an educational system that strengthens both sides of the brain. As sound healer Jonathan Goldman says, "It takes two wings to fly."

8. We are far more amazing than we realize. Group singing, with the powers I have spoken of, creates a sense of wonder and awe regarding our full potential. Music making helps us realize our magnificence.

9. Singing is our birthright. We are given ears and brains with which to listen and voices with which to make sounds. We are born into a universe in which harmony exists in all things. To sing and to make harmony is to become fully human.

10. Everyone who can hear can sing in tune. Openly solving children's out-of-tune singing problems shows that our problems can be solved—that we all have strengths and weaknesses, but with the work and support of others, most problems can be solved. Too many problems or differences are kept secret and hidden in the closet. Children get the wrong message when failure is seen as acceptable. Children see the correct message when they see teachers solving the problems of students in supportive ways. It gives every child the sense of confidence that if he or she has a problem, it too can be solved—the problem doesn't have to be treated as a hidden wound.

11. Folk songs are ecologically correct. You can use them again and again. You can also recycle them by changing them as you wish.

Music and Cultural Diversity

12. By singing the music of many cultures and of many styles, children learn to avoid making a distinction between good and bad music. This leads to a healthy appreciation for all music. The teacher who, on the other hand, condemns pop music is sending a message to students that it is okay to hate music.

   We need to honor the musical tastes of children. It is part of their self-identity. To insult their music is to insult them. By respecting rap and rock in all of their forms, we convey an openness to all music. Hopefully this openness will become part of the students' way of thinking. As they grow and their worlds expand, their tastes in music will expand. Their self-identity will grow to reflect their acceptance of new things. When we teach students to hate forms of music, on the other hand, these students don't grow to their fullest potential, and their chances of crossing cultural borders to enrich their lives are greatly diminished.

13. Singing songs of other cultures with an emphasis on feeling the deep traditions behind the songs gives children a strong emotional bond with each culture, as opposed to an intellectual, but incomplete, concept of what a culture is all about.

14. By examining the music of other cultures, students receive refreshing and diverse perspectives on what it means to be human. They see, for example, that in most cultures there is no separation between music, dance, art, and ritual or that in these cultures music is an essential part of daily life—without it, some believe, all things would cease to be. There are profound differences in how cultures view music. These views help to shape the identity of each culture. Seeing how other cultures define the human experience helps us to define our own lives.

15. By learning about other cultures, students absorb musical behaviors from these cultures that enrich their own lives. I, for example, have absorbed something from the mbira traditions of sub-Saharan Africa. The person who plays an mbira is not thought to be playing a solo because the instrument is considered to have a living presence of its own. The musician, therefore, is playing a duet. Now, when I sit down to play the music of Beethoven, I am playing a duet with the spirit of Beethoven.

16. When a child sings a spiritual such as "Swing Low, Sweet Chariot," it is easy for her to treat it like any other song. When this child, however, is taught about the perspective of those who created this spiritual, the slaves, the song takes on a whole new meaning. It becomes a song of pain, anger, and hope as well as great joy. The child can then better understand how ordinary actions in her life might seem very different from a different cultural perspective.

17. Students who sing music of other cultures begin to form antielitist frames of minds. The simple act of listening to other perspectives is important. But to actually celebrate other cultures and their differences through song is to transcend cultural elitism or me/them thinking to reach an antiracist way of thinking.

18. Students who explore the music of diverse cultures cease to see their own culture as the best culture and begin to see the interdependence of all cultures on this earth.

19. Celebrating the diversity of music is essential for students because they learn that the power of music does not lie in its universal qualities but in its differences. Diversity brings power in nature, in culture, and in music.

20. By singing the music of the earth and by celebrating this music with great power, we can transcend our normal frames of mind and enter a state of universal consciousness, a feeling that we are connected to all things. This magnificent sensation of interdependence is a feeling that, if felt by more people, could bring us together, creating a family of all humanity.

All-School Celebrations

21. People go to a gym for a workout of the body. People celebrate in musical performances as a workout for the mind, spirit, and body. This is true of both audience and performers.

22. In many cultures there is no separation between performers and the audience. When school assemblies involve everyone in singing and dancing, truly powerful celebrations are the result.

23. Powerful school celebrations help create a strong bond between the students and the school. School and education become part of the students' self-identity in a fun and positive way. I often encounter students who do not identify with their schools and who find negative bonds elsewhere. Singing celebrations can provide a needed sense of community. If the celebrations do not succeed in creating a bond, at least the students see the school as an environment in which the explosion of emotions (which is part of what celebrations are all about) is taken seriously.

24. As part of this, students learn that celebrating community and creativity is an essential part of learning.

25. A powerful singing celebration is a ritualized form of play. Children learn that play can take on serious dimensions and that they can be trusted participants in a very meaningful event.

26. By adding spice and variety to their lives, school singing celebrations show students that being a good student is as much hard work as it is serious play.

27. Preparing for a singing celebration requires both individual and group discipline. Giving students a sense of direction with specific goals is a great way to insure self-discipline on their part. Learning self-discipline at any age is an important process.

28. Simply by having singing celebrations, we demonstrate to children that celebrating in life is important.

29. There is a lot of talk in educational circles about striving toward excellence. Preparing for the singing celebration is a wonderful way to learn the value of excellence, but at the same time not to get hung up on an unattainable perfection. Striving for excellence means to work very hard toward letting the creativity, intelligence, and greatness within you shine out with the greatest intensity.

A flawless cold performance of music does not interest me. I greatly prefer a performance that sings of life's glory even if the performance has occasional disharmonies. If twenty children are on a stage singing, I want to see a shine radiating from the stage. That is excellence.

30. Reason #4 stated that children are like stars, they have a need to shine. We have all seen the faces of children after a school performance—the faces radiate with wonder and excitement. As with a star, the energy spreads out— you can't hold it back. Physicists call this the second law of thermodynamics, in which energy naturally spreads out rather than stays contained in one spot. The parents, teachers, and audience are touched by the children's energy as it shines out.

Compassion and Creativity

31. Singing is an act of compassion. When children sing, they make the world a more beautiful place.

32. Group singing requires respect and support for others, particularly if some are working on intonation problems. This respect for others is essential for education. The respect for others manifested in group singing eventually evolves to become a respect for the greater community, and ultimately, the earth. This compassion begins with each individual in response to those around him or her. The environment of supportive group singing is wonderful for teaching respect for others.

33. Singing compassionate music unites people in good causes. Powerless people can become powerful through group singing. Jailed antiapartheid activists in South Africa are told to be quiet, but instead they sing and the singing unites them, connecting them in a compassionate fire. For schools, singing compassionate music, particularly music of the great social struggles, unites students with problems around the world. Students begin to see that by celebrating and learning/feeling the music of social movements, they are being involved.

34. When students begin to feel the pain as well as the joy expressed in the music of many cultures suffering hardships, they will be more likely to become informed members of society. This is also true when students look at their own cultural histories, going back to times when survival was not as comfortable as it is today for the majority of North Americans.

35. Every sound we make is a new sound. To quote a song I wrote once, "I opened my eyes when I was born to discover the light. I opened my mouth when I was born to discover my voice. And the light and the voice will always be new, and the voice and the light will always be true." Every time we sing, we create something new. Like snowflakes that always have different designs, our songs always come out sounding new, something is always changing— our emotions, our energy—affecting the melodies, the rhythms, the mood— creating something that has never been heard before.

36. By encouraging the creative act of singing and all other creative expressions, we give children the signal that creativity is important in our lives.

Music and Learning

37. All of nature is full of patterns—things that make one object similar to another object. The bone structures of all mammals have the same basic patterns. There are also less obvious patterns such as the spiral patterns common to conch shells, pine cones, pine trees, and DNA molecules. Learning to recognize these patterns is an essential part of education. Music is the perfect vehicle for gaining this understanding. Music is full of patterns such as rhythmic patterns, melodic patterns, and patterns of harmony. In fact, when we break music down to its basic element, we find that it is all made of vibration—resonance. This resonance contains ratio patterns that are also found in the conch shell, the pine tree, and the DNA molecule.

As stated in reason #6 there are different types of intelligences. The patterns present in nature and music, even if not consciously recognized by students, have a tremendous impact on the students' learning. Musical intelligence helps the other intelligences. Cognitive skills such as counting, adding, and reading require a basic ability to recognize patterns. By making music, children are constantly making and learning patterns. This strengthens their ability to absorb other patterns in learning.

38. According to data by the Music Educators National Conference (MENC), American students who took music classes between 1987 and 1989 did twenty to thirty points better on both the math and verbal parts of the SATs than those with no classes in the arts at all.

39. Learning the words to many songs is great for the brain of the child. Learning other facts becomes easier.

40. Alphabet songs and counting songs have been a part of learning for young children for a long time. Teachers are beginning to use songs and raps with older students to more effectively teach history, math, and science. Besides being great for learning, singing during academic classes can be a lot of fun.

41. The research of Bulgarian psychiatrist Georgi Lozanov refers to multisensory learning (Brewer 1991, 228–31). The more senses that are involved in learning, the faster students will learn. He calls this accelerated learning. When music is integrated into other studies, students will learn their other studies faster. He prescribes recorded music to be played in the background during classes to improve student concentration.

42. Singing removes stress. This can be a help for any classroom (for both the students and the teacher).

43. When the teacher learns about the use of entrainment, many moods can be created among the students. By singing a slow song, the students will entrain with its pulse and enter a relaxed state of mind. Entrainment is used automatically by many experienced teachers. New teachers, baffled as to why they are having discipline problems, can learn the commonsense use of entrainment. Become aware of the many rhythms among individual students as well as in the whole class.

44. I have never seen a singing classroom that wasn't a happy classroom.

45. Younger children are developing physically. Songs with lots of movement help the children's coordination and involve them more completely.

46. Singing is something that students can look forward to doing every day.

47. Singing is a great transition vehicle between activities.

48. Have students sing before taking a test. They'll do better on the test. Their brains will be charged, particularly if their singing is resonant in tone. The reason students are very attentive after recess is because they have been yelling, talking, and chanting (patty cake, jump rope, etc.), thus charging the brain with resonance.

49. Teachers who learn the lesson of the resonant voice and who speak with resonance will hold the attention of students better than those who speak with dull or breathy voices.

50. Singing improves listening. The better students are at listening, the better they will do academically. Remember that the ancient Chinese word "sage" refers to a person who is wise because he or she listens well.

51. When younger children are making the transition from reading out loud to reading silently, those who have sung a lot will do better with the transition. They will be better at inner hearing and will be able to listen to words silently.

52. *Ob audire*, the root of the word *listen*, means "to reach out to sound." For students to reach out to sound, there must first be the desire or hunger for the sound. According to Dr. Alfred Tomatis, the hunger for sound stimulation begins in the womb. If it doesn't continue after birth, the child can lose much of his or her desire to learn.

53. Because balance is one of the ear's three functions, it is possible that singing (which involves listening) improves balance. This is another reason why movement needs to be part of singing.

54. Sound healers believe that the body has many rhythms, from brain waves to digestive cycles. They believe that music helps "tune" the body just as a mechanic uses sound to tune the engine of a car. There is, of course, much more involved with the human body.

55. When we sing in a group, the resonance of our voices massages our bodies inside and out.

56. Singing and sound may help to take away physical pain. When you drop a hammer on your foot, your immediate instinct is to make sound. That scream helps to take the pain away.

Music and the Emotions

57. Children are highly emotional. Singing creates a happy frame of mind. It is difficult to make singing an unhappy experience unless the teacher fails to create confidence in the singers. Group singing creates self-confidence.

58. Song leaders who create self-confidence in their students can then develop that confidence to create awe—a wonderful state of mind for children.

59. Singing is a highly emotional activity. Children need to use their emotions a lot—much more than most of us realize.

60. Many "problem" students are actually extremely emotional children who do not have the vent for all their emotions. Singing and celebration with the energy of stars is the perfect activity for these children. Many times, the child with discipline problems will receive Fs in all subjects except for the creative subjects such as art and music. This is not because they are more creative or less intelligent; it is because art and music give them a powerful way to let their emotions explode. Emotional intelligence is one of the intelligences that Howard Gardner speaks of. The problem child is often the one with a high emotional IQ.

61. Often, the emotions of children are powerful, yet simple—like on-and-off switches. The issue of fairness is crucial for this reason. With classroom singing, it is important for the children to know that there is no separation between talented and untalented singers.

Everyone is born with the potential to be a magnificent musician. When a child thinks she or he has no talent, it is as if her or his light switch has been turned off. This isn't fair and it isn't right.

62. We humans have a need for both normal and extraordinary experiences. Doing ecstatic music with children can be amazing for them. By twirling around for long periods of time, for example, children achieve something close to an ecstatic experience. It is something they do naturally, they seem to need amazing experiences—peak experiences. Music and celebration provide these experiences.

63. By encouraging classroom singing, especially emotionally charged singing, students get the message that the positive expression of emotions is okay in the educational environment.

64. Students who have trouble communicating their emotions often benefit from music making. This is one of the main features of music therapy—that music often communicates better than words. When we make music, we say something that all the dialogue in the world cannot express.

65. Music is a positive source of power for students as opposed to the many negative powers offered by such things as weapons and drugs. Students don't need to find power through violence. Music can provide tremendous power through its ability to energize the brain, body, and spirit and through its ability to bring communities together in exciting ways. Today's youth needs this message more now than ever before.

Of the sixty-five reasons listed above, no one reason jumps out as the most important. They are all important. Yes, schools can survive without art, music, and celebration. But they soon become prisons because no one will want to go there.

All the math, reading, and writing in the world won't make us smarter human beings. What makes us smart—in fact, what makes us geniuses—is that flame of intelligence within all of us. The environment that allows that light to shine at its brightest will create smarter human beings—better readers, writers, and mathematicians. That ideal learning environment is one where singing, which is celebration, is central to the curriculum.

A Look to the Future

The time is coming when music will develop possibilities
inconceivable now—a language so transcendent
that its heights and depths will be common to all mankind.

Charles Ives, *Essays Before a Sonata*

· THE GREAT American composer Charles
Ives, who wrote the above words, was a true sage, a man who listened to
the world with a great mind and a noble heart. I share his optimism in looking
forward to the promise of music's unlimited possibilities. For me, these amazing achievements will come about when we learn to utilize music's many
powers, both from the cross-cultural and biological perspectives.

For the millions of years of our human development, singing was central
to our evolution. This is a daring statement, one that I firmly believe to be
true. Until the entrance of the technological age, humans throughout the
planet sang as part of everyday life. But the comforts of modern technology
have been countered by a loss in firsthand experiences. We have CD players
and a million other ways to listen to music, but few of us actually make
music anymore. Furthermore, we tend to watch the world on TV rather than
experience it firsthand.

The TV has replaced the hearth as the center of the home. The days
when families gathered by the fire to sing old songs seems long ago. At
the turn of the century, secondary schools and colleges boasted glee clubs
populated with the vast majority of students participating. Community
choruses were everywhere. People sang on street corners. Every place of
worship was host to wonderful volunteer choirs. Lately, recordings of sacred
music have been competing in worship services with the original thing.

A hundred years ago, teachers were required to have musical training.
Every classroom teacher led songs. By the 1950s, music specialists began to

take over the music responsibilities. Now, music specialists everywhere are fighting to keep their positions. Music and singing are being cut from school curricula because they are incorrectly deemed as unnecessary. But many people are working hard to turn things around. As we learn more about music's amazing effect on the mind and body, we are beginning to find that education is empty without singing. As we learn more about the music of diverse cultures, we are learning that there are many ways to make music, each with its own powerful belief system deeply rooted in its cultural traditions.

There are many movements working toward the same goal. The many multicultural movements, the multiple intelligence movements, and the holistic and new paradigm movements are all working toward a reinvention of the human being—a human being with amazing capabilities—a human being capable of living in great harmony. Music and singing are the perfect vehicles for reaching this goal.

The proof is abundant—simply listen to Beethoven's Ninth Symphony. Hear the genius of what the universe can create when all of its powers work together.

Yes, this great "Ode to Joy" was created by the sun, moon, and earth with magnificent, interdependent, self-organizing creativity. It took the earth billions of years to get there, but it was worth the wait. Since 1825, Beethoven's work has stood as a pinnacle of human achievement, as something that could never happen again. And yet I believe that someday we humans will create works equaling the magnitude of Beethoven's Ninth Symphony on a daily basis. This new music won't sound like Beethoven, but it will have the transcendent power and the spiritual impact of Beethoven.

Armed with the new evidence of music's powers, people across North America are fighting for their state legislatures to make music and the arts mandatory at all levels of public school education. Many corporate and arts organizations are supporting this effort.

Adult community choral groups are on the rise. Many of these choral groups do not fit the old classical mold of the chorus. There are groups like the New York Streetsingers, a folk chorus started by Pete Seeger, which have two directors, one who draws repertoire from North America and from around the world, the other who directs music from Spanish-American cultures. All of their music is made with the West African sense of compassion—they are out to make the world a better place.

I direct a choral group called the Mystic Chorale. We don't do concerts, we do choral sing-alongs. And our music is drawn from the singing traditions of Eastern Europe, Southern Africa, Ireland, the Americas, and other parts of the planet.

The many gifted teachers I have met while leading school celebrations, have shared a genuine interest in increasing the amount of music their students receive. I have seen young people from preschools through high schools lit up by the energy of the singing celebration. There is a flame within them that will not go out.

Music is alive. It is part of the living process of nature. When we join voices to sing, we transcend our everyday state of being and become communities filled with awe and compassion, celebrating the fire of life and the light of our being.

This is the model for shaping the world. Listening. Creating. Sensing the wonder. Making harmony. The world is changing. As nations slowly adopt the interdependent model of one living earth and the family of all people, it will be music and singing that will bring us together.

Sing and shine on!

Listen and Sing

We do not sing one common song,
We do not speak one language,
But if we're going to get along
And throw out hate's old baggage,

Then people who are different
And powerful and strong
Should listen to each other
And then we'll get along.

Not listening is our problem now,
We think we've heard it all,
So listen to the voices
Of the children as they call,

I'm me, you're you.
We're great at our own thing,
But together we're a harmony,
So let's join voices and sing.

Appendix A

Suggested Tools and Supplies to Help You in Teaching Songs

Cassette Tape Recorder

If you don't read music, the tape recorder is a great way to remember new songs. Simply sing the songs into the tape recorder and label the tape. If there's a song in this book that you can't read, bring the book and the tape recorder to someone who can read music. Record the song.

Music publishers like World Music Press, Home-Spun Tapes, SingOut! and others offer tapes to accompany the songbooks so that those who wish to remain in the aural tradition can learn the songs by listening to them.

Many teachers ask their students to sing along with the tape recorders. I urge you *not* to do this. It goes against everything I have talked about in this book.

Sometimes you may hear a recording of a song you want to do, but you want to teach it higher than it is on the recording. You may want to sing it into the tape recorder in the higher key. Note the pitch name of the first note (see pitch pipe). Note: There are special cassette tape recorders where you can slow down or speed up the sound, thus making the song lower or higher.

If you ever write songs either by yourself or with students, the tape recorder is a perfect way to remember how the songs go.

When you are getting ready to teach a round, it is a good idea to sing the round into the tape recorder. Record three or four repetitions of the round without stopping between repetitions. Then practice singing the song as a round over your taped voice. Sometimes songs like "Amazing Grace" can be turned into rounds. Figuring out when the second voice comes in, however, can be tricky. Record the song a few times, then sing over your taped voice, experimenting with your entrances. Remember that most songs can not be turned into rounds. The tape recorder is a good way to find out which songs work and which don't.

You may want to add percussion parts or vocal percussion parts over a song. You may want to add a harmony or a drone. The tape recorder is a perfect tool for figuring these things out. (With time, you can learn to do these things in your head.)

The tape recorder is also a great accessory for the classroom. Playing music in the background during study times can be very good for the student's concentration. Allow students to bring their favorite tapes in to listen to during break times. This adds to their sense of ownership of the music.

You can record your students' singing. Listen to it later to figure out how to make them sound better. Or play the recording to the students and ask them for their opinion.

Three-Ring Notebook for Collection of Songs

Become a song collector. Constantly add new songs to your notebook. Collecting songs can become a great student activity as well. When you enter a new song, be sure to write down where you heard or found the song. You may want to return to the source later on. Many people are storing songs on computers now. This is especially helpful if you plan on using overhead projectors to display the words, as you will have the words on the computer ready to print out.

Pitch Pipe

Pitch pipes are circular handheld harmonicalike instruments. The pitches of the scale (C, D, E, F, etc.) are labeled around the rim. Blow the pitch softly and listen carefully to find your starting note. All music stores sell pitch pipes. Tuning forks only give you one note. It is apt to be a more accurate note than the pitch pipe, but if the tuning fork gives an A pitch, you may have trouble finding an F pitch. The tuning fork is recommended, therefore, for those with backgrounds in music theory.

Music Manuscript Paper

If you can read music, you can learn to write it as well. Keep some music manuscript paper handy for writing down new songs when you hear them.

Hand Drum

The handheld drum is the only instrument you might want to use in leading songs. You don't need to use guitars and autoharps or pianos, for that matter.

Children sound better, in the long run, without those instruments. Use the hand drum to keep a steady beat. Drums are very powerful. They add a lot to songs, even songs that don't usually use drums.

There are different kinds of hand drums. Music suppliers sell tunable hand drums. They have little tuning pegs around the rim. These are all-purpose drums because drums without the tuning pegs are susceptible to changes in weather. The Irish bodhran (pronounced boron with accent on second syllable) has a gorgeous sound that can be made higher by pushing the inside of the drum head with the hand that holds the drum. There is a special two-headed stick used to hit the bodhran. Many folk music stores sell bodhrans.

The Native American hand drum is an extremely powerful instrument. A leather-tipped stick or mallet is used to hit the drum. The Native American drum may be a little harder to find. If you do find one, treat it with great respect. Know that it contains the spirit of the animal it is made of. Do not let children bang mindlessly on it. Treat it with reverence. Be sure not to buy a cheap tourist imitation drum. The company Honey Rock, mentioned in the Resource Guide, has a great variety of hand drums for sale.

Percussion Instruments to Share with Singers

It is fun to have an assortment of simple percussion instruments that students can share. Shakers, hand drums, sticks, cowbells, tambourines are all easy to find. There are many more exotic instruments you can buy as well. I often cut dowels at about ten inches, then sand the ends. They make excellent stick percussion instruments. I like to pass out quieter percussion instruments, reserving the cowbells and tambourines for especially boisterous songs. It is, of course, essential that students learn to play percussion instruments at a reasonably soft volume.

Overhead Projector

The bigger overhead projectors are hard to store, but are less expensive. The portable ones are convenient. Always have an extra bulb and an extension cord handy. The plastic overhead sheets run through any copy machine, even through laser printers if you have access to one. Cardboard frames are available for the overheads. Having words projected on a wall or screen is excellent for those following the words as it keeps their heads up—a better posture for singing. Also, not making copies of the songs is good for the environment.

The Newsprint-Size Easel

Many teachers prefer to write the words to songs on newsprint and then mount them on easels for everyone to learn. Song sheets can later be posted on the walls or hung from the ceiling.

Other

The computer is being used in our classrooms in amazing new ways. I use an overhead projector. I am constantly juggling hundreds of songs in separate cardboard frames. Eventually, I hope to have an accessory that lays on top of the projector, projecting the words from my laptop computer through the accessory and onto the screen.

Eventually, you will be able to sing a melody into a computer and have it print out the melody. You will also be able to have the computer read a melody for you.

There are already many interesting CD-ROM interactive discs available. You can see and hear music being performed along with the written music. As it's playing, you can ask questions or receive historical and cultural backgrounds.

Eventually, encyclopedic volumes like the *Groves Dictionary of Music* will be available on either CD-ROM or through Internet. We will be able to hear, see, and read about the music of any culture on earth. And we will be able to do this in the classroom.

Through the Internet we can learn about the music of any culture on this planet.

For composing music in the classroom, there is nothing more fascinating these days than a computer hooked up to an electronic midi keyboard. The possibilities are staggering.

And while the computer and other technologies will continue to help and amaze us, they will never be able to replace simple firsthand experiences like singing.

Appendix B
Powerful Song Suggestions with Sources and Age Recommendations

You should, of course, use your own judgment as to what age is appropriate for each song. Also, when the age recommendation says six and up, that applies to everyone over the age of six, including adults.

"Ain't Gonna' Let Nobody Turn Me 'Round" (civil rights song). Ysaye Barnwell and George Brandon, eds. From *Singing in the African American Tradition*, available from Homespun Tapes. Simplified: ages 6 and up.

"All Work Together." Woody Guthrie. Available from *Sing Out!* Publications. Ages 4 and up.

"Bless Oh Lord Our Country Africa" ("N'Kosi Sikeleli Afrika," anthem of the ANC). From World Music Press. For chorus melody: ages 6 and up. For full harmony: ages 12 and up.

"Bridges." Bill Staines. From *First Million Miles*. Ages 10 and up.

"Cumbayah." Sweet Honey in the Rock. From *All For Freedom*, available from Music for Little People or Ladyslipper Catalog. Ages 6 and up.

"Donna Donna" (Yiddish theatre song). From *Rise Up Singing* songbooks (with tapes), available from *Sing Out!* Publications. For the chorus: ages everyone. For the verses: ages 8 and up.

"The Earth Is Our Mother" (Contemporary Native American). From Libana songbooks, available from Ladyslipper Catalog. Ages 4 and up.

"Follow the Drinking Gourd" (African American folk song). From *Rise Up Singing* songbooks (with tapes), available from *Sing Out!* Publications. Ages 8 and up.

"Freedom Calypso." Sweet Honey in the Rock. From *All For Freedom*, available from Music for Little People or Ladyslipper Catalog. Ages 6 and up.

"Freedom Is Coming." Anders Nyberg, ed. From *Freedom Is Coming*, South African songbook and tape, available from Dove Music or World Music West. Simplified: ages 6 and up. Original: ages 11 and up.

"Garden Song." David Mallet. From *Rise Up Singing* songbooks (with tapes), available from *Sing Out!* Publications. For chorus: ages 5 and up. For verses: ages 8 and up.

"Go Down Moses" (spiritual). From *Rise Up Singing* songbooks (with tapes), available from *Sing Out!* Publications. Ages 8 and up.

"Good Night Irene." Ledbelly. From *Rise Up Singing* songbooks (with tapes), available from *Sing Out!* Publications. Ages 6 and up.

"Green Grow the Rushes" (English folk song). From *Rise Up Singing* songbooks (with tapes), available from *Sing Out!* Publications. Ages 6 and up.

"Had I a Golden Thread." Pete Seeger. From *Rise Up Singing* songbooks (with tapes), available from *Sing Out!* Publications. Ages 6 and up.

"Harriet Tubman." Walter Robinson. From *Rise Up Singing* songbooks (with tapes), available from *Sing Out!* Publications. Ages 8 and up.

"Hava Nashira" (Hebrew round). From *Rise Up Singing* songbooks (with tapes), available from *Sing Out!* Publications. Ages 10 and up.

"Here Comes the Sun." George Harrison. From *Rise Up Singing* songbooks (with tapes), available from *Sing Out!* Publications. For chorus: ages 5 and up. For verses: ages 8 and up.

"I Feel Like Goin' On." Eleanor D. Bell-Stokes and Andre Sonny Woods. Ysaye Barnwell and George Brandon, eds. From *Singing in the African American Tradition*, available from Homespun Tapes. Ages 12 and up. Simplified: ages 8 and up.

"If I Had a Hammer." Pete Seeger and Lee Hays. From *Rise Up Singing* songbooks (with tapes), available from *Sing Out!* Publications. Ages 6 and up.

"Ise Oluwah" (Yuroba chant, West Africa). Sweet Honey in the Rock. From *All For Freedom*, available from Music for Little People or Ladyslipper Catalog. Ages 10 and up.

"Jig Along Home." Woody Guthrie. From *Rise Up Singing* songbooks (with tapes), available from *Sing Out!* Publications. Ages 4 and up.

"Kwaheri" (Kenya). From Libana songbooks, available from Ladyslipper Catalog. Ages 8 and up.

"Little Red Caboose." Sweet Honey in the Rock. From *All For Freedom*, available from Music for Little People or Ladyslipper Catalog. Ages 5 and up.

"Make a Little Motion." Sweet Honey in the Rock. From *All For Freedom*, available from Music for Little People or Ladyslipper Catalog. Ages 4 and up.

"The Midnight Special." Ledbelly. From *Rise Up Singing* songbooks (with tapes), available from *Sing Out!* Publications. Ages 6 and up.

"Neesa Neesa" (Seneca). From Libana songbooks, available from Ladyslipper Catalog. Ages 4 and up.

"Never Turning Back." Pat Humphries. From *Rise Up Singing* songbooks (with tapes), available from *Sing Out!* Publications. Ages 8 and up.

"Now I Walk In Beauty" (Hopi text). Music by Gregg Smith. From Libana songbooks, available from Ladyslipper Catalog. Ages 8 and up.

"Now I Walk In Beauty" (Navaho). Bryon Burton. From *Moving Within the Circle*, available from World Music Press. Ages 6 and up.

"Place in the Choir (All God's Critters)." Bill Staines. From *Rise Up Singing* songbooks (with tapes), available from *Sing Out!* Publications. For chorus: ages everyone. For verse: ages 6 and up.

"River." Bill Staines. From *Rise Up Singing* songbooks (with tapes), available from *Sing Out!* Publications. For chorus: ages 5 and up. For verses: ages 8 and up.

"Roll On Columbia." Woody Guthrie. From *Rise Up Singing* songbooks (with tapes), available from *Sing Out!* Publications. Ages 8 and up.

"Silvie." Ledbelly. From *All For Freedom*, available from Music for Little People or Ladyslipper Catalog. Ages 4 and up.

"Simple Gifts" (Shaker hymn). From *Rise Up Singing* songbooks (with tapes), available from *Sing Out!* Publications. Ages 6 and up.

"So Glad I'm Here." Sweet Honey in the Rock. From *All For Freedom*, available from Music for Little People or Ladyslipper Catalog. Ages 4 and up.

"Somagwaza" (South African). Ysaye Barnwell and George Brandon, eds. From *Singing in the African American Tradition*, available from Homespun Tapes. Ages 12 and up.

"The Storm Is Passing Over (Courage My Soul)." Charles A Tindley. Ysaye Barnwell and George Brandon, eds. From *Singing in the African American Tradition*, available from Homespun Tapes. Ages 12 and up.

"Sweet Honey in the Rock." Bernice Johnson Reagon. From *Compositions: One*, available from Ladyslipper Catalog. Ages 12 and up.

"Swing Low, Sweet Chariot" (spiritual). From *Rise Up Singing* songbooks (with tapes), available from *Sing Out!* Publications. Ages: everyone.

"This Land Is Your Land." Woody Guthrie. From *Rise Up Singing* songbooks (with tapes), available from *Sing Out!* Publications. Ages: everyone.

"This Little Light of Mine" (spiritual). From *Rise Up Singing* songbooks (with tapes), available from *Sing Out!* Publications. Ages: everyone.

"Thuma Mina." Anders Nyberg, ed. From *Freedom Is Coming*, South African songbook and tape, available from Dove Music or World Music West. Ages 11 and up.

"Tumbalaika" (Yiddish folk song). From the Harvard Hillel Sabbath Songbook, available from Tara catalog. For chorus: ages 6 and up. For verses: ages 10 and up.

"Tzena Tzena" (Hebrew round). From *Rise Up Singing* songbooks (with tapes), available from *Sing Out!* Publications. Ages 8 and up.

"Vine and Fig Tree." Shalom Altman. From *Rise Up Singing* songbooks (with tapes), available from *Sing Out!* Publications. Ages 8 and up.

"Wade in the Water." Ysaye Barnwell and George Brandon, eds. From *Singing in the African American Tradition*, available from Homespun Tapes. Ages 6 and up.

"The Water Is Wide" (English folk song). From *Rise Up Singing* songbooks (with tapes), available from *Sing Out!* Publications. Ages 8 and up.

"We Are Marching." Anders Nyberg, ed. From *Freedom Is Coming*, South African songbook and tape, available from Dove Music or World Music West. Simplified: ages 6 and up. Original: ages 11 and up.

"We Will Not Give Up the Fight." Anders Nyberg, ed. From *Freedom Is Coming*, South African songbook and tape, available from Dove Music or World Music West. Simplified: ages 6 and up. Original: ages 11 and up.

"With A Little Help From My Friends." John Lennon and Paul McCartney. From *Rise Up Singing* songbooks (with tapes), available from *Sing Out!* Publications. Ages 8 and up.

"Woyaya (We'll Get There)" (contemporary South African). Ysaye Barnwell and George Brandon, eds. From *Singing in the African American Tradition*, available from Homespun Tapes. Ages 12 and up.

"Yellow Submarine." John Lennon and Paul McCartney. From *Rise Up Singing* songbooks (with tapes), available from *Sing Out!* Publications. Ages for the chorus: everyone. Ages for the verses: 6 and up.

"Yonder Comes Day." Available from World Music Press. Ages 8 and up.

"Zum Gali Gali." (Israeli round). From *Rise Up Singing* songbooks (with tapes), available from *Sing Out!* Publications. Ages 8 and up.

Resource Guide

American Choral Directors Association
(Choral Journal)
P.O. Box 6310
Lawton, OK 73506

*Periodical and support organization for
choral directors.*

American Orff-Schulwerk Association
(The Orff Echo)
P.O. Box 391089
Cleveland, OH 44139-8089

*Periodical and support organization for
choral directors.*

Drumbeat Indian Arts
4143 N. 16th St.
Phoenix, AZ 85016
602-266-4823

*Excellent source for Native American
music, especially Navaho.*

Dekay's House of Music
39 Thrift St.
San Francisco, CA 94112

*Black Gospel music distributor, both re-
cordings, octavos, and song books. They
also have how-to books on Gospel style
piano playing.*

Folk-Legacy Records, Inc.
Sharon, CT 06069

*They offer a variety of traditional music
recordings.*

Folkways, The Whole Catalog
Smithsonian/Folkways Mail Order
414 Hungerford Dr. Suite 444
Rockville, MD 20850
Fax: 301-443-1819

*Great old and new folk, ethnic, jazz etc.
recordings.*

GIA Publications, Inc.
7404 S. Madison Ave.
Chicago, IL 60638
800-GIA-1358
Fax: 708-496-3828
http://www.giamusic.com

They have the best songbook/tape sets of songs for ages one through five.

HaZamir Music Publications
(Distributor of much of their music:
Transcontinental—see below)
35 Garland Rd.
Newton, MA 02159
http://www.zamir.org

Jewish choral music by Josh Jacobson, David Burger and others. Highly recommended.

Homespun Tapes
Box 694
Woodstock, NY 12498

How-to tapes and videos on learning folk and jazz instruments. Also contains tapes on yodeling, singing in harmony as well as Ysaye Maria Barnwell's exceptional set, Singing in the African American Tradition.

Ladyslipper Catalog
P.O. Box 3124-R
Durham, NC 27715

Recording and song book distributor for women's music.

MENC: The National Association for
Music Education
1806 Robert Fulton Dr.
Reston, VA 20191-4348
703-860-4000

Music Educators Journal is their magazine for music teachers. They also publish excellent guidebooks and videos on a variety of subjects including multicultural and multi-sensory music teaching issues.

Music For Little People
Box 1460
Redway, CA 95560
800-246-4445

Wonderful children's recordings by Tom Chapin, Sweet Honey in the Rock, Sally Rogers, Ladysmith Black Mambazo and many others.

Organization of American Kodály Educators
National Office
1612 - 29th Ave South
Moorhead MN 56560
218-227-6253

The Kodály approach uses singing and music literacy skills with the use of solfeggio—do, re, mi syllables. Wonderful published folk materials and educational conferences.

Perry Enterprises, Inc.
P.O. Box 395
Silver Springs FL 34489
1-800-52-SAY-NO

Robert Perinchief writes drug education music for children. He also publishes Honor Your Partner Songs, a fine collection of partner songs, two or more songs that can be sung at the same time.

Primarily A Cappella
P.O. Box D
San Anselmo, CA 94979
415-455-8602
e-mail: harmony@netcom.com

*Catalog of all kinds of a cappella record-
ings and books of arrangements.*

Revels Inc.
One Kendall Square, Building 600
Cambridge, MA 02139

*They publish wonderful folk songs in book
and octavo form. Also many recordings.*

Sing Out! The Folksong Magazine
P.O. Box 5460
Bethlehem, PA 18015-0460
215-865-5366

*Quarterly folk music magazine. They also
publish and distribute excellent folksong
books and Rise Up Singing, a song book
with tapes, containing over 1,200 very
singable songs. Highly recommended.*

The Society for Ethnomusicology, Inc.
Univ. of Michigan, 48109
Ann Arbor, MI 48109
(Ethnomusicology—the SEM journal)

*Academic journal for the study of music
and culture. The books and essays are
meticulously researched, but not always
easy for the non-ethnomusicologist to
understand. The society hosts regional
meetings with very interesting presenta-
tions on the music of many cultures.*

Tara Publications
PO Box 707
Owings Mills, MD 21117
800-TARA-400
Fax: 800-TARA-403

*Tara publishes song books representing
the great diversity of music within the
Jewish tradition.*

Transcontinental Music Publications
838 5th Avenue
New York, NY 10021
212-249-0100

*Choral music from many Jewish
traditions, both sacred and secular.*

World Music Institute
49 West 27th St. Suite 930
New York, NY 10001
212-545-7536
www.heartheworld.org

*Concerts, videos, books and recordings
of music from all parts of the earth.
Catalog.*

World Around Songs
Rt. 5 Box 398
Burnsville, NC 28714
828-675-5343

*Small-format folk song collections,
available since the Fifties, with music
of many cultures appropriate for sing-
a-longs with people of all ages. They
have some great collections of rounds
and canons.*

Bibliography

I. Music and Culture

Anderson, William M., and Patricia Shehan Campbell, eds. 1989. *Multicultural Perspectives in Music Education*. Reston, VA: The Music Educators National Conference (MENC).

A good introduction.

Banks, James, 1989. *Multicultural Education: Issues and Perceptions*. Boston: Allyn and Bacon.

Along with the Sleeter and Grant book, Making Choices for Multi-Cultural Education, *this is an excellent book for understanding the issues of multiculturalism in education. Recommended.*

"Becoming Human Through Music, The Wesleyan Symposium on the Perspectives of Social Anthropology in the Teaching and Learning of Music," 1985. At Wesleyan University in Middletown, CT, 8/6-8/84. Reston, VA: Music Educators National Conference (MENC).

These articles offer an excellent argument for multiculturalism in music education. The link between music and cultural identity is made very well. Recommended.

Berliner, Paul. 1978. *The Soul of the Mbira, Music and Traditions of the Shona People of Zimbabwe*. Berkeley: University of California Press.

A fascinating look at the "thumb piano" and the amazing cultural framework behind it. Along with Chernoff's book, African Rhythm and African Sensibility, *the book changes the way you think about music.*

Blacking, John, 1973. *How Musical Is Man?* Seattle: University of Washington Press.

Out of print, but for educators interested in the issue of how music is taught in diverse cultures, this book is well worth the search.

Bragaw, Don and W. Scott Thomson, eds. 1992. *Multicultural Education, A Global Approach.* NY: The American Forum for Global Education, 45 John Street, Suite 908, NY, 10038.

"Growing Up Complete: The Imperative for Music Education." 1991. The Report of The National Commission of Music Education (MENC). 1902 Association Drive, Reston, VA 22091.

Excellent collection of essays, many related to how children in cultures around the world learn about music. The essays then ask the obvious question, "If it works for others, will it work for us?"

Marre, Jeremy, and Hannah Charlton. 1985. *Beats of the Heart, Popular Music of the World.* New York: Pantheon Books.

Books and videos. Excellent look at many styles of music ranging from Pentecostal Preachers in Appalachia to the excellent Beats of Resistance, on the Pop music of South Africa. Recommended.

Moyers, Bill, Don Marino, ed., Elena Mannes, Prod. and Dir., *Amazing Grace* (Video), Public Affairs Television Inc. for WNET New York and WTTW in Chicago.

Video about the hymn "Amazing Grace." It explains the power of the song by looking at its history as well at the diverse cultural traditions that have embraced the song. Recommended.

The New Grove Dictionary of Music and Musicians. Ed. by Stanley Sadie. 2000. London: Macmillan Publishers Ltd.

An extraordinary multi-volume resource on all music from all cultures.

Page, Nick, 1995. *Music As A Way of Knowing.* Stenhouse Publishing, P.O. Box 360, York, ME 03909 (800-988-9812; fax: 207-363-9730)

This book is part of a series dedicated to the integration of the arts into the classroom—how to teach science, history etc. using music.

Parker, Alice. 1976. *Creative Hymn Singing.* Chapel Hill, NC: Hinshaw Music, Inc. P.O. Box 470, Chapel Hill, NC 27514.

——. 1991. *Melodious Accord: Good Singing in Church.* Chicago: Liturgy Training Publications, 1800 N. Hermitage Ave., Chicago, IL 60622.

These two books by composer Alice Parker need to be read by every church musician or anyone interested in how to breath new life into old music.

Toop, David. 1998. *The Rap Attack 3: African Jive to New York Hip Hop.* Boston, MA: South End Press.

If you know nothing about rap, read this book. You will definitely respect rap as an ancient musical tradition. Recommended.

II. Music and the New Paradigm

Brewer, Chris, and Don C. Campbell. 1991. *Rhythms of Learning: Creative Tools for Developing Lifelong Skills.* Tucson, AZ: Zephyr Press, P.O. Box 13448, 85732-3448.

This book discusses entrainment and other rhythm principles to be used in the future of education. Recommended.

Dissanayake, Ellen. 1988. *What is Art For?* Seattle: University of Washington Press.

———. 1992. *Homo Aestheticus: Where Art Comes From and Why.* NY: The Free Press.

These two books and others by Dissanayake are written with a scientist's respect for accuracy. They combine the studies of anthropology, evolutionary psychiatry, and aesthetics in a fascinating way. Recommended.

Gardner, Howard. 1983. *Frames of Mind.* NY: Basic Books.

Gardner is the leading champion of the concept of multiple intelligences.

Gardner, Kay. 1990. Sounding the Inner Landscape. Stonington, ME: Caduceus Publications.

One of the better books on music healing.

Gilmor, Timothy M., Paul Madaule, and Billie Thompson, eds. 1989. *About The Tomatis Method.* Toronto: The Listening Centre Press.

On the many uses of the Tomatis Method for healing and for education. See Tomatis, The Conscious Ear, *below.*

Hart, Mickey, with Jay Stevens. 1990. *Drumming at the Edge of Magic.* San Francisco: Harper.

Grateful Dead drummer Mickey Hart has compiled this book on the effect of drumming on the people or many cultures. See also his book, Planet Drum.

Nash, Grace C., and Janice Rapley. 1990. *Music in the Making: Optimal Learning in Speech, Song, Instrument Instruction and Movement for Grades K-4.* Van Nuys, CA: Alfred Publishing Co.

Grace Nash has been active since the 1950s in showing the importance of music in all education. Her counting/rhythm books have become classics.

Swimme, Brian. 1984. *The Universe is a Green Dragon: a Cosmic Creation Story.* Santa Fe: Bear & Company.

Easy to read interpretation of new paradigm science and how it affects our way of thinking.

Tomatis, Alfred A. 1991. *The Conscious Ear: My Life of Transformation Through Listening.* Barrytown, NY:

Station Hill Press.

The Tomatis method is controversial, but worth investigating. He believes that music charges the brain.

Wallace, Rosella R. 1992. *Rappin' and Rhymin': Raps, Songs, Cheers, and SmartRope Jingles for Active Learning.* Tucson, AZ: Zephyr Press.

Fun teacher activity book using rap and other spoken styles to teach classroom subjects.

III. Songbooks

Adzenyah, Abraham Kobena, Dumisani Maraire, Judith Cook Tucker. 1996. *Let Your Voice Be Heard! Songs from Ghana and Zimbabwe.* Danbury CT: World Music Press.

19 Call and response, game songs, story songs and multipart songs from Ghana and Zimbabwe for use with all grade levels. Includes extensive cultural context. Book/audio CD set.

Ashley, Bryan. 1984. *I'm Going To Sing: Black American Spirituals*, vols. 1 & 2. New York: Atheneum.

Ashley's wood block illustrations are superb.

Barnwell, Ysaye, and George Brandon. 1989. *Singing in the African American Tradition, Choral and Congregational Vocal Music.* Woodstock, NY: Homespun Tapes, Ltd.

Six tapes where Ysaye Barnwell teaches the harmonies one part at a time—her way of keeping the songs

within the aural tradition. With great background information. Highly recommended!

Behan, Dominic. 1973. *Ireland Sings.* NY: Music Sales Corporation.

Political and other songs from Ireland including Behan's "The Patriot Game."

Blood-Patterson, Peter, ed. 1988. *Rise Up Singing.* Bethlehem, PA: A Sing Out Publication, PO Box 0460, Bethlehem PA, 18015.

The best collection of folk song lyrics around. Tapes available.

Burton, Bryan. 1993. *Moving Within the Circle: Contemporary Native American Music and Dance.* Danbury, CT. World Music Press.

Book/audio CD set. Highly recommended!

Carawan, Guy, and Candie Carawan, 1989. *Ain't You Got a Right to the Tree of Life? The People of John's Island, South Carolina-Their Faces, Their Words, and Their Songs.* Athens, GA: The University of Georgia Press.

Fascinating look at a fascinating culture. Many of the songs are easily learned, improvised upon and memorable.

——. 1990. *Sing for Freedom: The Story of the Civil Rights Movement Through Its Songs.* Bethlehem, PA: Sing Out Corporation.

With excellent historical information.

Diliberto, Rosella. 2000. *Welcome to Mussomeli: Children's Songs from an Italian Country Town*. Danbury CT: World Music Press.

Easy-to-learn songs, recipes and cultural context from Rosella's Sicilian childhood. Book/audio CD set.

Fowke, Edith, and Joe Glazer, eds. 1960. *Songs of Work and Freedom*. Garden City, NY: Dolphin Books, Doubleday and Company, Inc.

Now classic collection of songs.

Get America Singing, Again!: 45 Sing-along Songs (and *Get America Singing, Again! 2*) edited by Will Schmid and MENC (Music Educators Natonal Conference) with a forward by Pete Seeger. Published by Hal Leonard Corporation.

Songs every child should know and will love to sing.

Gold, Ben-Zion. 1992. *Harvard Hillel Sabbath Songbook: One Hundred Sabbath Songs with All the Sabbath Blessings*. Gordine.

Wonderful collection of sacred songs.

Goseyun Wilson, Chesley, and Ruth Longcor Harnisch Wilson, Bryan Burton, 1994.*When The Earth Was Like New: Western Apache Songs and Stories*. (Book/audio CD set) Danbury, CT: World Music Press.

A book that shows great respect to the powerful living legacy of Apache culture.

Hirschorn, Linda. 1989. *Gather Round: New Hebrew Canons, Rounds and Musical Settings*. Cedarhurst, NY: Tara Publications.

Exciting collection, especially for those looking for new paradigm and/or feminist songs within the Jewish tradition.

Jenkins, Ella. 1968. *The Ella Jenkins Songbook*. NY: Oak Publications.

Great collections of children's songs from around the world adapted by the greatest children's song leader of them all. Highly recommended. Ella Jenkins has many recordings.

Johnson, James Weldon, and J. Rosamond Johnson. 1977. *The Book of American Negro Spirituals*. NY: Da Capo Press, Inc.

Superb collection by the author and composer of "Lift Every Voice and Sing."

Jones, Bessie, and Bess Lomax Hawes. 1987. *Step It Down: Games, Plays, Songs and Stories from the Afro-American Heritage*. Athens, GA: University of Georgia Press.

Great collection for anyone interested in historical accuracy in singing African American children's songs. A classic.

Langstaff, Nancy, and John Langstaff, eds. 1985. *The Christmas Revels Songbook: In Celebration of the Winter Solstice*. Boston: David R. Godine, Publisher, Inc.

Includes Wassail songs and other non-Christmas seasonal songs.

————. 1978, 1986. *Sally Go Round The Moon: And Other Revels Songs and Singing Games for Young Children.* Cambridge, MA: Revels Publications.

Creative collections of fun songs. Revels also sells recordings of English ritual music from many seasons as well as a collection of sea chanteys.

Nyberg, Anders, ed. *Freedom Is Coming: Songs of Protest and Praise from South Africa for Mixed Choir.* Chapel Hill, NC: Walton Music Corporation.

Book and recording of SATB songs and chants. Great for grades six and up. With words in Zulu and English. Highly recommended!

Orozco, Jose-Luis, ed. Ill. by Elisa Kleven. *De Colores and Other Latin-American Folk Songs for Children.* New York, NY: Dutton Children's Books, 1994.

Beautifully illustrated collection.

Perrinchief, Robert. *Honor Your Partner Songs.* Silver Springs, FL: Perry Enterprises, Inc.

A great book of partner songs (songs that can be sung simultaneously).

Schafer, Andre., 1994. *My Harvest Home: A Celebration of Polish Songs and Customs.* Danbury CT: World Music Press. (Book/audio CD set.)

Seeger, Pete. 1985. *Abiyoyo.* NY: MacMillan.

This is an illustrated children's story adapted by Pete Seeger. Children can sing-a-long with the song "Abiyoyo" as the book is read to them. Delightful!

Seeger, Pete. 1983. *Where Have All the Flowers Gone: A Singer's Stories, Songs, Seeds, Robberies.* Bethlehem, PA: Sing Out Corporation.

Pete Seeger has written an autobiography using his own songs and others as a way of telling his life story. Highly recommended.

Seeger, Ruth Crawford. 1948. *American Folk Songs for Children.* NY: Doubleday.

A now classic collection of songs with an excellent introduction on the folk song tradition. This is still in print and an important part of any elementary music educator's library.

Shehan Campbell, Patricia, Ellen McCullough-Brabson, Judith Cook Tucker. 1994. *Roots & Branches, A Legacy of Multicultural Music for Children.* Danbury, CT: World Music Press.

A must book /audio CD set for any classroom teacher who wants to teach songs of many cultures. Highly recommended!

Songs of Zion. 1981. Nashville: Abingdon Press.

Fantastic collection of African American Hymns, Spirituals, and Gospel Songs—with historical backgrounds for each style.

Staines, Bill. 1980. *If I Were a Word, Then I'd Be a Song*. Sharon, CT: Folk-Legacy Records, Inc.

Contemporary folk songs like "All God's Critters Got a Place in the Choir," and "River."

Stoloff, Bob. *Scat! Vocal Improvisation Techniques*. Brooklyn, NY: Gerard and Sarzin Publishing Co. 146 Bergen St. Brooklyn, NY 11217 (book/audio CD)

Sweet Honey In The Rock. 1989. *All For Freedom.* (Recording) Redway, CA: Music For Little People.

Great African and African-American songs for children including "Sylvie," "Kumbaya," "Little Red Caboose," "Ise Oluwah" and others.

Weber, Sol, ed. 1948. *Rounds Galore! Captivating Rounds, Old and New*. Distributed by Sing Out! Co.

The best collection of rounds. Recommended. An informal collection of rounds as well as a CD or cassette tape are available.

For Nick Page's complete fifty-page *Resource Guide* see his web site:
www.nickmusic.com
The web site also contains:
•A List of Nick Page's Choral publications
•Information on his workshops and song leading availability
•The Nick Page Songbook CD
•Essays on Music

More Songs for Group Singing

The following pages offer you several more tried and true songs from a variety of traditions to get you rolling. You'll also find a few pages of music manuscript. Jot down gems that cross your path before you forget them!

Amigos

Words and Music by Judith Cook Tucker

Translate the verses into the languages of your school or community.

There's A River Flowin' In My Soul

Slow Gospel

by Rose Sanders (used by permission), as sung by Jane Sapp

There's a ri-ver flow-in' in my soul.
heart.
mind.

There's a ri-ver flow-in' in my soul.
heart.
mind.

and it's tell-in' me that I'm some-bo-dy. There's a

(last time through, repeat "There's a river flowin'" several times)

ri-ver flow-in' in my soul. There's a
heart.
mind.

Somebody Prayed

Medium Gospel

African-American Hymn as sung by Jane Sapp

Some-bo-dy sang for me. Had me on their mind,
marched
prayed

took the time and sang for me. ____
marched
prayed

I'm so glad they sang. I'm so glad they sang.
marched. marched.
prayed. prayed.

I'm so glad they sang for me. Some-bo-dy
marched
prayed

The Duchess at Tea

Medium, Four-Part Round   Music by Pat Shuldham-Shaw, Lyrics by Woodrow Wilson

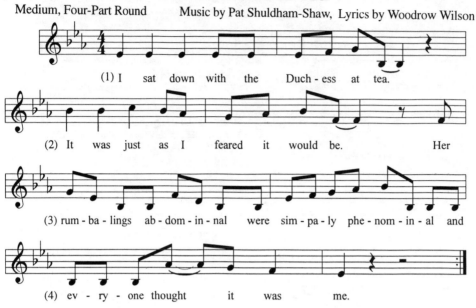

(1) I sat down with the Duch-ess at tea.

(2) It was just as I feared it would be. Her

(3) rum-ba-lings ab-dom-in-nal were sim-pa-ly phe-nom-in-al and

(4) ev-ry-one thought it was me.

Cockles And Mussels

In Dub-lin fair ci-ty where the girls are so pret-ty, twas
She was a fish-mon-ger and sure twas no won-der, for
She died of a fe-ver and no one could save her and

there that I first met sweet Mol-ly Ma-lone, and she wheeled her wheel-
so were her fa-ther and mo-ther be-fore, and they each wheeled their
that was the end of sweet Mol-ly Ma-lone, and her ghost wheeled her

bar-row through streets broad and nar-row cry-ing, "Cock-les and Mus-sels, a-
bar-row
bar-row

CHORUS

live, a-live - o." A - live, a-live - o, a - live, a-live - o, cry-ing,

"Cock - les and Mus-sels, a - live, a - live - o." She

Silvie

Slow or Fast

by Huddie Leadbetter, better known as Leadbelly

Bring me lit-tle wa-ter Sil - vie. Bring me lit-tle wa-ter now

Bring me lit-tle wa-ter Sil - vie. Ev'-ry lit-tle once in a while.

Sil-vie come 'a run - ning, buck-et in her hand, ___

Won't you fetch me lit-tle wa - ter fast as you can. ___

O Hal'lwe

Traditional Native American: Nanticoke tribe of Delaware, USA
A Women's honoring song. The words "o hal'lwe" mean "strong oak tree."

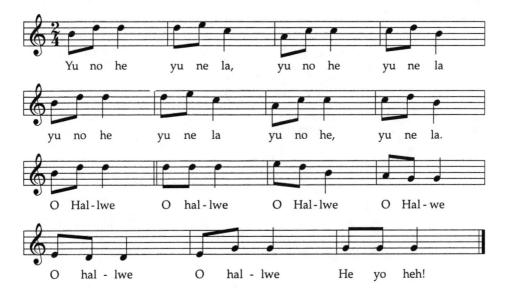

Yu no he yu ne la, yu no he yu ne la

yu no he yu ne la yu no he, yu ne la.

O Hal-lwe O hal-lwe O Hal-lwe O Hal-we

O hal-lwe O hal-lwe He yo heh!

Dowidzenia

Four-part Canon. Sing in Polish.

Words and Music © 1996 by Andrea Schafer

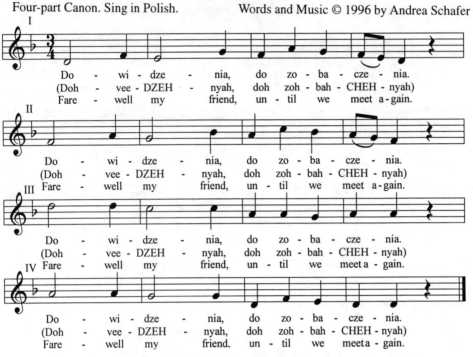

Do - wi - dze - nia, do zo - ba - cze - nia.
(Doh - vee - DZEH - nyah, doh zoh - bah - CHEH - nyah)
Fare - well my friend, un - til we meet a - gain.

Do - wi - dze - nia, do zo - ba - cze - nia.
(Doh - vee - DZEH - nyah, doh zoh - bah - CHEH - nyah)
Fare - well my friend, un - til we meet a - gain.

Do - wi - dze - nia, do zo - ba - cze - nia.
(Doh - vee - DZEH - nyah, doh zoh - bah - CHEH - nyah)
Fare - well my friend, un - til we meet a - gain.

Do - wi - dze - nia, do zo - ba - cze - nia.
(Doh - vee - DZEH - nyah, doh zoh - bah - CHEH - nyah)
Fare - well my friend, un - til we meet a - gain.

La Macchina del Capo

Traditional Italian

as sung by Rosella Diliberto

Translation: The boss's car has a hole in its tire. Let's all fix it with chewing gum!

La mac-chi-na del ca-po ha_un bu-co nel-la

gom-ma La mac-chi-na del ca-po ha_un bu-co nel-la

gom-ma La mac-chi-na del ca-po ha_un bu-co nel-la

gom-ma Ri-pa-ria-mo ri-pa-ria-mo la col chew-ing gum!